Department of Education and Science
Department of Education for Northern Ireland
Welsh Office

Assessment of Performance Unit

Mathematical Development

Secondary Survey Report No. 2

by
D D Foxman
M E Badger
R M Martini
P Mitchell

Report on the 1979 secondary survey from the National Foundation for Educational Research in England and Wales to the Department of Education and Science, the Department of Education for Northern Ireland and the Welsh Office.

London
Her Majesty's Stationery Office

ISBN 0 11 270517 0

Contents

Tables

Figures

Acknowledgements

The monitoring team at the NFER would like to thank the large number of people who played a part in enabling the survey reported here to take place and who contributed to the work involved in producing this report.

We are again indebted to the schools which participated. Many of the heads and teachers in these schools made helpful comments on the content and presentation of the test materials. We should also like to thank the LEAs who nominated teachers to be testers in the practical mathematics survey. These teachers (listed in Appendix 3) wrote extremely valuable critiques of the tests which will make a substantial contribution to the development of this innovative form of assessment.

The monitoring surveys require careful administrative and coordinating procedures. These were the responsibility of Mrs B Bloomfield as head of the Monitoring Services Unit and her staff based at the NFER. They were responsible for all matters pertaining to contact with the LEAs and the schools which took part in the survey. The statistical analysis of the results was guided by members of the NFER Technical Committee and, in particular, by Mr B Sexton and his colleague Mr P Smedley.

A number of colleagues at the NFER, members of the Monitoring Group, made helpful comments on the initial draft of the report as did Dr I Wells of the Northern Ireland Council for Educational Research. Members of APU Committees, the Steering Group on Mathematics, the Advisory Group on Statistics and the Consultative Committee, have read and discussed the initial draft and their recommendations have greatly contributed to the final draft of the report.

Successive versions of the text and various amendments have been typed with much patience and skill by our secretary Mrs A Watson and typists Mrs J Fisher and Miss K Maychell; and were assembled by our clerical assistant Mrs R James.

Summary of report

1 This report is the second in a series which will aim to present a national picture of the mathematical performance of 15 year olds in England, Wales and Northern Ireland. It covers the survey carried out in November 1979 by the National Foundation for Educational Research on behalf of the Assessment of Performance Unit. The overall picture of performance which is presented is very similar to that obtained in 1978. A few statistically significant differences were identified but these may have arisen by chance. In these circumstances, the report does not contain any comparisons with the results of the 1978 secondary survey.

Second secondary survey (Chapter 1)

2 This survey is the second in an initial programme of five annual surveys aimed at establishing a firm baseline of data on the mathematical performance of 15 year olds. With further periodic monitoring after that, it should become possible to identify trends in performance and to pinpoint areas worthy of more detailed examination. In the 1979 secondary survey, written tests were administered to a representative national sample of about 12,750 pupils in the age group in England, Wales and Northern Ireland. These tests were the same as those used in 1978 except that a few items were amended to take account of comments made by teachers whose pupils had taken part in the first survey. A sub-sample of just over 1,000 pupils also took a practical test and a further sub-sample of about 900 pupils completed an attitude questionnaire. The survey results of individual pupils, schools or local education authorities are not identified.

The practical tests (Chapter 2)

3 The practical interactive mode of assessment allows the tester to explore pupils' reasoning and understanding of mathematical ideas in an atmosphere which is less formal than the written test situation. Some pupils respond better in this less formal atmosphere and particular benefit is gained by pupils with reading difficulties. Ten practical topics were assessed in 1979 within the broad categories of number, geometry, measures, and probability and statistics (see Table 2.1). Two of the topics, symmetry and probability, had not been included in the 1978 survey. As in 1978, testers were provided with a script for each topic but two important changes were made in 1979: (i) the scripts included a coding

schedule which provided guidance on pupils' likely responses, although testers were asked not to consider these codes as a strait-jacket for their recording; (ii) testers were encouraged to probe to a greater extent the methods and strategies used by pupils if these were not immediately clear from the responses given.

4 The outcomes of the practical tests are reported by means of tables and verbal reports. Seven topics are reported ranging from the use of a calculator to the construction of pinboard triangles. For each topic percentage scores are given for all pupils and the results of boys and girls are compared. The chapter also includes a brief discussion of the correlations between the practical topics and the written tests.

The written tests: item clusters (Chapter 3)

5 Whereas the report on the first secondary survey presented and commented on the broad picture provided by the written test results, the emphasis in this report has been to analyse and comment on selected areas of mathematics in greater depth. This chapter contains some interpretations of pupils' responses to clusters of items of related content. The item clusters are analysed in terms of success rate, rate of omission and the incidence of the most common errors made in the case of those items which were attempted. The differences in these proportions are then related to the differences in the items' content and context in an attempt to identify those features which are most likely to affect item difficulty. The analyses also give some indication of the particular strategies used by pupils to tackle questions.

The written tests: sub-category scores and background variables (Chapter 4)

6 Although the written tests used for the 1979 secondary survey were the same as those used in 1978, there were some significant changes in the marking strategies which were adopted. In order to take account of these changes, which in some cases affected the average difficulty of a test or even a whole sub-category, test scores are scaled rather than expressed as a percentage of correct responses. In this way, allowance can be made for the varying difficulties of each test arising from the different assortment of items contained in them.

7 The pattern of performance in each sub-category of the written tests is described in relation to six background variables. Five of these are characteristics of the schools in the sample, and data are also reported for boys and girls separately. The overall mean scaled scores obtained by

pupils in each grouping of the background variables are illustrated in Table 4.1 and shown graphically in Figures 4.2–4.6. Analysis revealed that overall performance and performance in relation to the background variables were very similar to that reported for 1978. However, the report stresses that trends cannot be detected from the results of only two surveys. Valid and meaningful comparisons will only be possible when further surveys have been carried out and evidence gathered to show whether differences between years are due to chance variation or are part of a general long-term trend.

Attitudes towards mathematics (Chapter 5)

8. The 1979 secondary survey included, for the first time, an attitude questionnaire which was completed by a sub-sample of about 900 pupils. As well as being a discipline within the school curriculum, mathematics is also perceived as a series of topics. Pupils are, therefore, likely to have not only a predisposition towards the subject as a whole but also positive or negative feelings about its constituent components. The attitude questionnaire was designed in such a way as to investigate both these aspects of attitude; it also asked pupils questions about their attitudes to school subjects in general.

9 General attitudes towards mathematics were measured by pupils' responses to 34 statements expressing opinions about it in terms of liking, usefulness and difficulty. An analysis of responses revealed that girls found mathematics more difficult than boys; they enjoyed it less and perceived it as less useful. As far as attitudes to specific topics were concerned, boys tended to find the activities more useful and interesting than girls did. Comparisons between the attitudes of 15 and 11 year olds revealed that the former, particularly girls, perceived mathematics as being less important than did the younger pupils. 15 year old pupils also saw less value than 11 year olds in most of the topics and enjoyed mathematics less. Whilst 11 year old pupils believed that mathematics would play an important part in their future careers, 15 year olds were dubious about its relevance to their everyday life.

The survey results (Chapter 6)

10 The pattern of results obtained in this survey was similar to that described in *Secondary Survey Report No. 1* in relation to data from the 1978 survey. This similarity in the general picture applied to mathematics as a whole and also within the bands of the background variables. The results have added some more detail to the picture of performance already reported by giving some tentative indications of the different levels of

understanding that pupils have of the various mathematical concepts. Comparisons of the errors made by 15 and 11 year olds in response to the same or similar items revealed, for example, that when asked to compare decimal numbers less than 1 almost as many 15 year olds as 11 year olds (more than 20 per cent) appeared to ignore the decimal point. However, survey data are subject to random fluctuations and no valid conclusions about trends in performance can or should be drawn from the results of only two surveys.

11.   Development is continuing in the existing assessment procedures and new assessment materials are being piloted. The major area of current item development is concerned with problems, applications and investigations.

1 Second secondary survey

The aims of the mathematics surveys

1.1 The initial programme of the APU in relation to the mathematics line of development will consist of a series of five annual surveys of the performance of 11 and 15 year olds. The purpose is to establish a firm base line of data for the identification of any trends which may develop during or subsequent to the initial five years.

1.2 In order to meet these objectives, a detailed picture of performance is being built up over successive years. The aims are different from those of the more familiar kind of assessment procedures such as examinations, which focus on the individuals taking the tests by placing them in order of merit or by deciding whether they have attained specified criteria of competency such as a pass mark or stated objectives of learning.

1.3 In the APU surveys, individual pupils take the tests but individual performances are merged into the total picture which is the object of the assessment. It is not necessary for each pupil in the sample to take the same test, nor is there any need for all pupils in the target age group to be tested. Statistical procedures are available to enable the overall picture to be validly predicted from a sample which, although small in relation to the target population, is nevertheless representative of it.

[1] *Mathematical development. Secondary survey report No. 1.* HMSO, 1980, price £6.60

1.4 Full details of the sampling procedure were given in the first secondary survey report[1]. It is designed to produce a national representative sample of 15 year olds for the written tests and representative sub-samples for the practical mathematics and attitude assessments. It is not designed to make comparisons between individual pupils, schools or authorities, and consequently such comparisons cannot be validly made with the data which are obtained.

Secondary survey 1979

1.5 This report is an account of the results of the second survey of the mathematics performance of pupils in schools in England, Wales and Northern Ireland who attained the age of 16 years during the year 1979 – 80.

1.6 The second survey took place in November 1979 and was conducted by the NFER on behalf of the Assessment of Performance Unit (APU) at the Department of Education and Science (DES). The work is sponsored by the DES, the Welsh Office and the Department of Education for Northern Ireland.

1.7 As in 1978, written tests were administered to a representative national sample of pupils in the age group. Separate sub-samples of the main sample also took either practical tests or attitude questionnaires. The attitude questionnaires were administered for the first time to this age group.

1.8 In 1979 the size of the main sample was about 12,750 pupils. About 8,000 pupils were from English schools, 2,000 from Welsh schools and 2,750 from schools in Northern Ireland. About 650 schools were involved in the survey.

1.9 Each of the pupils in the sample was given one of the 25 written tests. These tests were the same as those used in 1978 except that about fifteen of the six hundred or so items were amended to take account of comments from teachers of pupils in that survey. These changes were mainly typographical and were intended to make the presentation of the items clearer. Each written test consisted of a different selection of items from three of the fifteen sub-categories of mathematics in the assessment framework (see Figure 1.1).

1.10 In the practical mathematics survey 10 topics were assessed, 7 of them identical to those used in 1978. The remaining 3 topics were new or amended from the previous year. The tests were administered by 27 experienced teachers of the age group who were nominated by their local authorities and trained to administer the tests by the NFER monitoring team. Up to five pupils were tested in each of the 227 schools in the practical survey sub-sample.

1.11 In the attitude questionnaires pupils were asked to respond to statements about their enjoyment of mathematics, how difficult they found it and how useful they thought it to be. They were also asked to attempt items representative of some mathematical topics and to indicate whether they found them interesting, difficult and useful. Six pupils from each of 170 schools in the sub-sample took attitude questionnaires in 1979.

New features of the reporting

[1] *Mathematical development. Secondary survey report No. 1.* HMSO, 1980, price £6.60.

1.12 The first secondary survey report[1] presented and commented on the full width of the picture provided by the results, with a consequent lack of some detail. The emphasis in this second report has been to analyse and comment on selected areas of mathematics in greater depth. The topics chosen for extended discussion have been sampled from each of the five main categories of the curriculum framework.

1.13 In Chapter 2, which is concerned with the results of the practical tests, detailed accounts are given of topics from the categories geometry (visualisation), measures (mass, length, angles), probability and statistics (probability and data representation), and number (calculators and fractions). Chapter 3 is an account of the responses given to some clusters of items of related content in the written tests. They are from the categories geometry (angles), number (place value), algebra (conventions) and measures (ratio and proportion). The reporting of both written and practical tests is orientated more towards pupils' understanding of mathematical concepts and procedures on this occasion than in the first secondary survey report.

[1] For a full description of the scaling procedure see *Mathematical development. Primary survey report No. 2.* HMSO, 1981, price £5.80. Appendix 3, pp 98–103.

1.14 A new feature of the reporting of the results of the written tests within bands of the background variables in Chapter 4 is that the sub-category scores for 1979 are given in scaled units. Scaling[1] is a method of making allowance for the different difficulties of the 25 tests resulting from the different collection of items used in each test.

The assessment framework

1.15 The framework is the same as that used in 1978 but has been amended in one respect: 'applications' no longer appears among the categories of learning outcomes, and categories of context (mathematical, everyday, and other subject) have been added to those of content and outcome. The 'applications of number' sub-category is now seen as testing number concepts and skills in an everyday context: this is a change in classification only and not in the assessment materials. The introduction of 'context' as a separate categorisation is intended to stress the cross-curricular aspect of the monitoring. The context categories are not seen as having clear-cut boundaries and they will be used in the reports to contrast pupils' performance on individual items which have different settings but similar mathematical content.

Figure 1.1   *Assessment framework*

Content \ Outcome	Concepts Skills	Outcomes of Problem solving and Investigating	Attitudes	
Number	Concepts Skills Applications of number	Included in 1980 in practical tests and from 1981 in written tests	Liking, difficulty and utility of mathematics as a subject	Interest, utility and difficulty of specific mathematical topics in the curriculum
Measures	Unit Rate and ratio Mensuration			
Algebra	General algebra Traditional algebra Modern algebra Graphical algebra			
Geometry	Descriptive geometry Modern geometry Trigonometry			
Probability and Statistics	Probability Statistics			

Each outcome can be assessed in either written or practical (interactive) modes. The content can be set in mathematical, everyday or other subject contexts.

1.16 The framework for assessment of pupils at age 15 has the same main categories as that for age 11. However, there is a different distribution of sub-categories at each age level, for example, at age 11 there is greater emphasis on number.

2 Practical tests

The practical tests

2.1 Mathematical thinking is involved in a variety of both theoretical and practical tasks. In these tasks mathematical ideas can be communicated in various ways: through writing and reading symbols, diagrams and words; by constructing and manipulating models and apparatus and by talking about mathematical situations.

2.2 The practical interactive mode of assessment was developed in order to assess a number of these activities more appropriately than is possible with the more formal pencil and paper tests. Practical tests are administered to pupils individually by experienced teachers of the age group who are nominated as testers by their Local Education Authority. Pupils have an opportunity to ask for clarification of the tasks they are set and to retract or amend their initial responses. The assessors, on their part, can obtain information on pupils' understanding by observing the methods they use to undertake a task, or by asking them for descriptions and explanations of what they have done.

2.3 In contrast to the written test situation, some pupils respond better in the less formal, more socially interactive atmosphere of the practical assessment. Pupils who have reading difficulties derive particular benefit from this type of test situation.

2.4 As in 1978, testers were provided with a script for each topic employed in the survey. They were instructed to read the items to the pupil and record the responses made together with any interaction which followed the initial response. In contrast to 1978 the interview scripts were arranged so that a coding schedule was printed opposite each page of script. The codings listed the range of responses which had been encountered during pilot work or, in the case of topics used previously, during the 1978 survey. The codes provided guidance on the likely responses, but testers were asked not to make them a strait-jacket for their recording. Free recording enabled some of the codings to be adjusted after the survey in the light of the further experience gained of pupils' responses.

2.5 Another development for this survey was that testers were asked to focus more on pupils' methods and strategies than they had done in 1978. The scripts included instructions to probe for the method used if it was not clear from what the pupil did or said how he had obtained his result.

2.6 Opposite is an extract from the script of the fractions topic. (The codings in the boxes were counted as acceptable responses.)

Present F(3) $(\frac{1}{2} + \frac{1}{4})$
"What is the answer to this?"

_____
_____
_____
_____

$3/8$

Probe for method
"Tell me how you got your answer."

_____

Changed ½ to ¾, then added together bottom line, then top line.

6.   ANSWER AND METHOD:

A.   0.   No response

1. $\frac{3}{4}$

6. $\frac{1}{6}$

7. $\frac{2}{6}$

8. $\frac{1}{3}$

9.   Other

M.   0.   No response

1. $\frac{1}{2} = \frac{2}{4}$, $\frac{2}{4} + \frac{1}{4} = \frac{3}{4}$ oral

2. $\frac{1}{2} + \frac{1}{4} = \frac{2+1}{4} = \frac{3}{4}$ written

3.   Just know it

6.   Added tops, added bottoms

9.   Other

2.7 Item 6 instructs the tester to present to the pupil the sheet, labelled F(3), on which was printed $\frac{1}{2} + \frac{1}{4}$. The tester then read the words printed in italics "What is the answer to this?" and the pupil responded with "$\frac{3}{8}$". This response was recorded on the right hand section of the interview sheet. Since the method was not clear the tester asked the pupil how the answer had been obtained and received the explanation recorded on the right-hand section of the interview sheet.

Design of the practical survey

2.8 Table 2.1 shows the ten topics which were used in the survey. Symmetry and probability were new topics, developed for use in 1979. The calculators topic was revised and extended from the 1978 version, while the remaining seven topics had only minor changes from the 1978 survey.

2.9 The pupils who were given a practical test were a sub-sample of those taking the written tests. The practical survey took place over a two-week period in November 1979 and the dates were chosen so that approximately half the pupils took the practical test before the written test whilst the remainder took the written test first. In this way any effect caused by the order of administration was balanced.

Table 2.1   *Practical topics used in the 1979 secondary survey*

Main content category	Topic	Subcategory of curriculum framework
Number	*Calculators* approximation, use of calculator, inverse operation	Number concepts Number skills
	Fractions add, multiply, divide by computation and illustration	Number concepts Number skills
Geometry	*Visualisation* constructing 3D models from diagrams, reflection	Descriptive geometry
	Symmetry properties of lines of symmetry by folding and using a mirror	Descriptive geometry
Geometry and Measures	*Angles* estimating and measuring acute, obtuse and reflex angles, angles of triangle	Descriptive geometry Unit measures
	Length estimating and measuring straight and curved lines rectangle and circle	Descriptive geometry Unit measures
Measures	*Mass* use of balance	Unit measures
	Area units of area, irregular shape	Unit measures
	Capacity/Volume estimation using small and large containers	Unit measures
Probability and Statistics	*Probability* basic concepts, recording of results	Probability

*These topics are discussed in this Chapter.

2.10 The ten topics were assembled into ten tests (see Table 2.2) so that each pupil took three topics. No test contained the same three topics and each topic appeared in a different position in each test. In this way, any learning or "settling down" effects on topics were controlled.

2.11 Testers visited up to ten schools each and tested a maximum of five pupils in each school. On any particular day of the survey half the testers were administering the even-numbered tests and the other half the odd-numbered tests. In addition, the order of the tests was different on each day, so that any effects arising from the order in which pupils came for testing were balanced.

Table 2.2 *Topics in each test*

Test Number	Topic 1	Topic 2	Topic 3
1	Symmetry	Capacity/Volume	Area
2	Mass	Symmetry	Probability
3	Fractions	Mass	Capacity/Volume
4	Calculators	Fractions	Symmetry
5	Angles	Calculators	Mass
6	Length	Angles	Fractions
7	Visualisation	Length	Calculators
8	Area	Visualisation	Angles
9	Probability	Area	Length
10	Capacity/Volume	Probability	Visualisation

2.12 Local Education Authorities nominated 27 testers to administer the survey. Twenty-three were from England, two were from Northern Ireland and two from Wales. Pupils in Wales had the option of being tested in Welsh.

2.13 The testers attended a two and a half day residential briefing conference held in September 1979. They were shown videotapes of each topic, practised filling in the interview sheets and took part in simulations of the interview situation. After the conference testers administered the tests to pupils in their own schools in order to gain further experience before the survey. The scripts from these practice sessions were checked and comments sent back to testers in order to standardise the testing procedure.

2.14 In all about 1150 pupils were tested in 227 schools, with about 330 pupils taking each topic.

Results of released topics

2.15 The results from seven of the ten topics used in the 1979 survey are reported in this section: the results of the others will be given in a subsequent report. In addition, the pinboard topic described here was used in the 1978 survey only but was not chosen for discussion in the report on that survey.

2.16 For each item the responses given by pupils both before tester intervention and after it were coded. The amount and type of the prompting by testers were also coded. The proportions of pupils giving specified responses are reported and data is also given separately for boys and girls, mainly to supplement the evidence on sex differences given in Chapter 5, *Attitudes towards mathematics*. A few of the differences between boys' and girls' results are indicated as being statistically significant at the 5 per cent level: the meaning of such differences is discussed in Appendix 2.

2.17 **Tables** of the results are provided at the end of the discussion on each topic except for the probability and pinboard topics. The percentages given in the tables are those for acceptable responses before tester intervention.

Probability

2.18 This topic was developed for the 1979 survey. It sets out to assess pupils' understanding of some aspects of the concept of probability. Pupils' performance in making clear and appropriate records of the outcome of a series of chance events was also tested.

The coin: Two outcomes

Prediction

2.19 The first set of questions concerned the possible outcomes of tossing a coin. Pupils were asked to predict the most likely number of heads that would result from 10 tosses of a coin. 60 per cent of the 319 pupils who took this topic said 5 heads was the most likely outcome because there was an equal chance of a head or a tail each time. A further 10 per cent also predicted 5 heads but could not give an adequate justification for their answer; for example, some said that $10 \div 2$ gave 5 without giving an explanation of how this related to the question.

2.20 Just over 15 per cent gave a specific number of heads other than 5. Often these pupils were influenced by their past experience, for example: *"It's usually heads when I do it."*

2.21 Other pupils considered the result would depend on how the coin was tossed or which face was uppermost to begin with. The following responses were typical:

> *"No way of telling, depends how hard you flick it."*
> *"10 times because you've got heads facing you."*
> *"Depends on which side you had it to begin with."*

Experiment: recording and generalisation.

2.22 The tester then tossed the coin 10 times and the pupil was asked to record the results so that the number of heads would be known at the end of the 10 tosses. Over 40 per cent of pupils wrote headings and used tally marks to record the results. A similar proportion recorded the results in order, e.g. H H T H T T - - - - -. A few pupils noted only when the coin landed heads, thus omitting to keep count of the number of tosses.

2.23 When the outcome was 5 heads, a number of pupils who had given sound reasons why 5 heads was the most likely outcome expressed surprise that their predictions were confirmed. Typical responses to the question *"Are you surprised by what happened?"* were:

> *"A little bit – the theory doesn't always come out in practice."*
> *"Yes, it usually doesn't work out for me."*

2.24 Few pupils expressed surprise when there was a 6 – 4 split in the number of heads and tails. Over 40 per cent attributed the results to luck and stated that any number of heads was possible. Examples of comments made after 4 or 6 heads were obtained were:

"It's just luck – any number of heads can come up."
"Not really surprised. It never worked out when we did probabilities."

2.25 Some pupils appreciated that equal numbers of heads and tails could not always be expected with a small number of tosses, for example:

"It was only 10 tosses. If it had been a few thousand then it would be about even but it will differ for small numbers."

2.26 With more extreme results some pupils commented that equal numbers of heads and tails should have been obtained, but most said any result was possible. On the whole, with the more extreme outcomes pupils tended to express surprise or refer to past experience or comment on the way the coin was thrown, whereas results close to 5 heads usually produced explanations of a more mathematical nature.

2.27 Pupils were than asked whether the results would be the same in a repeated run. 71 per cent said they would not be the same, 8 per cent thought they would be and the rest were undecided.

The die

2.28 The remaining part of the topic concerned the possible outcomes with one or two dice. Pupils were first asked how many numbers there were on a die and then in how many ways it could land. 94 per cent answered these questions correctly, revealing high familiarity with the die. Unsuccessful pupils were told the correct answer, as this was needed for subsequent questions.

2.29 Around 65 per cent gave the theoretically correct result when asked how many times each number might be expected to appear in 18 throws of a die. Most explained their answer by saying that $18 \div 6$ gave 3, though only 17 per cent added that each number had an equal chance as justification for their prediction.

2.30 This differs from the explanations given for 5 heads being the most likely outcome in 10 tosses of a coin, when 60 per cent of pupils said each outcome was equally likely.

2.31 Some pupils responded with a specific number of times other than 3. Over 10 per cent said each number would appear twice and others predicted 4 or 5 times for each outcome. In certain cases this was the result of arithmetical errors or a misunderstanding of the question, although further questioning of some pupils revealed that they meant each number should come up at least twice, rather than exactly twice, for example:

Pupil: *"Twice"*
Tester: *"Why?"*
Pupil: *"Because there are 18 throws and only 6 numbers and therefore one number has got to come up at least twice."*

2.32 Some pupils said it was impossible to predict, and examples of responses in this category are:

"It depends – you could get all 6's or all 3's."
"You can't say. They're always different every time you throw the dice."
"You don't know. It's a square and it goes in different directions."

2.33 Other pupils thought some numbers would come up more often than others and examples of such responses are:

"I think 5 would come up a few times, so would 4, 3 and 2, but 1 and 6 wouldn't come up as often."
"6 would not come up very often. It's got more paint on it so it will be at the bottom."

2.34 Pupils were then asked to throw the die 18 times and record the results so that afterwards they could say how many times each number came up. 55 per cent used tally marks to record their results although some of these did not keep track of the number of throws and often made checks to ensure that precisely 18 throws were made. Of the 45 per cent who merely listed the outcomes as they appeared, half failed to keep track of the number of throws.

2.35 Around 30 per cent expressed surprise at their results but over half were not surprised, commenting that any set of results would be possible.

2.36 The following exchanges illustrate the range of responses

Example 1
Pupil A had predicted 3 of each number and her results were:

Number	1	2	3	4	5	6
Frequency	2	4	2	3	5	2

Tester: *"Are you surprised?"*
Pupil A: *"No not really."*
Tester: *"Why not?"*
Pupil A: *"3 of each is only theory. The theory is more accurate over larger samples."*

Example 2
Pupil B predicted 1 and 6 would not come up as often as the others. Her results were:

Number	1	2	3	4	5	6
Frequency	3	3	3	1	5	3

Tester: *"Are you surprised?"*
Pupil B: *"Surprised 6 came up so many times."*
Tester: *"Why?"*
Pupil B: *"Because when I play games with dice it normally takes a long time to get a six."*

2.37 When asked how many times each number would turn up in 300 throws, pupils were less confident than with their responses for 18 throws. Over 10 per cent did not respond and nearly 55 per cent gave the theoretically correct result but many said the outcome could not be predicted. Others based their answers on personal experience or on the results they obtained with 18 throws, for example:

> "I'd expect 5 and 6 about 100 times each, 4 about 20 times and the rest 10 times."
> "I don't know but 4 would come up more than anything."

Those who felt some numbers would come up more often than others frequently gave predictions which did not total 300.

2.38 Pupils were then asked whether it was easier to guess what number would turn up on a die or whether a coin would land on heads or on tails. 92 per cent said the outcome of tossing a coin was easier to predict than throwing the die. Most gave as their reason the fact that there were only 2 alternatives on the coin, although a few mentioned the higher probability of predicting the outcome with a coin.

2.39 The final section of the topic concerned the possible scores with 2 dice. 52 per cent knew what scores could be obtained, but some included 1 as a possible score while others just said there were 12 different scores. Just over half thought all scores were equally likely. Fewer than 15 per cent gave a full explanation that the middle scores were more likely because there were several ways of getting them. Some pupils who replied that certain scores came up more often than others were only using past experience in dice games to justify their response. Here are two records of the questions:

Example 1

Tester:	"Do you think any of these scores are likely to come up more often than any of the others?"
Pupil A:	"Might get 7 a lot."
Tester:	"Why?"
Pupil A:	"Because I used to play Monopoly and 7 used to come up a lot – don't know why."
Tester:	"How can you get a score of 7?"
Pupil A:	"5 and 2, 4 and 3 or 6 and 1."
Tester:	"Which score will come up least often?"
Pupil A:	"Don't know really."

Example 2

Tester:	"Do you think any of these scores are likely to come up more often than any of the others?"
Pupil B:	"2 and 12 are less likely to come up."
Tester:	"Why?"
Pupil B:	"It's rare to get 2 ones or 2 sixes together."
Tester:	"Which is most likely to come up?"
Pupil B:	"Any of the rest."

[1]319 pupils took this topic.

2.40 Many testers and pupils[1] enjoyed this topic. Testers commented that it allowed pupils to demonstrate their intuitive ideas about probability, whilst pupils seemed to prefer the more informal nature of the topic, with questions not apparently having any mathematical basis. While some pupils had clearly studied the topic before, others considered the whole subject a matter of chance or referred to personal experience to justify their results.

Comparisons with primary topic

[1] Mathematical development. Primary survey report No. 2. HMSO, 1981, price £5.80.

2.41 The probability topic used in the 1979 primary practical is fully described in the second primary survey report[1]. It was essentially the same as the secondary version except that primary pupils were not asked about the possible outcomes with two dice.

2.42 Nearly 65 per cent of primary pupils said 6 heads would be the most likely outcome if a coin were tossed 12 times. 70 per cent of secondary pupils gave the correct answer for 10 tosses. After tossing the coin pupils were asked whether they thought the same results would be obtained in a second experiment and similar responses were made at both age levels.

2.43 Almost half the primary pupils gave the theoretically correct result when asked how many times each number would come up in 24 rolls of a die. This compares with 65 per cent of 15 year olds, but it should be noted that the secondary question referred to 18 rolls of a die. Some of the difference in success rates may be due to secondary pupils' greater competence in arithmetic compared with primary pupils rather than in their understanding of the concept.

2.44 When asked which was easier to predict, the outcome of tossing a coin or the outcome of throwing a die, nearly 90 per cent of primary pupils gave the correct response, almost as many as at the secondary level.

2.45 Methods of recording the results of the experiments differed since primary pupils were offered a choice of plain or squared paper and this produced a wide range of methods. The majority of primary pupils chose squared paper and although few drew a graph or chart, most utilised the squares in some way to record their results.

Angles

2.46 This topic tested pupils' ability to estimate and measure acute, obtuse and reflex angles, and their knowledge of simple angle properties related to right angles, angles on a straight line and angles in a triangle.

2.47 As a first task, pupils were presented with a sheet showing a right angle (Figure 2.1) and were asked to estimate the size of the angle.

85 per cent identified the angle as 90, although 4 per cent of these did not mention the word "degrees". A few pupils commented that the angle looked like 90°, but since it was not labelled in the usual way (⌐), they gave responses such as 89° or "a bit more than 90°"

Nearly 5 per cent estimated the angle as 45°. Unsuccessful pupils were told the angle was 90° as this information was required for reference purposes in subsequent questions.

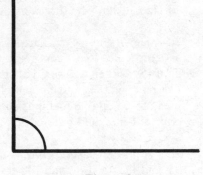

Figure 2.1

2.48 Pupils were then presented with a sheet with three angles drawn on it (Figure 2.2) and asked to estimate the size of each angle.

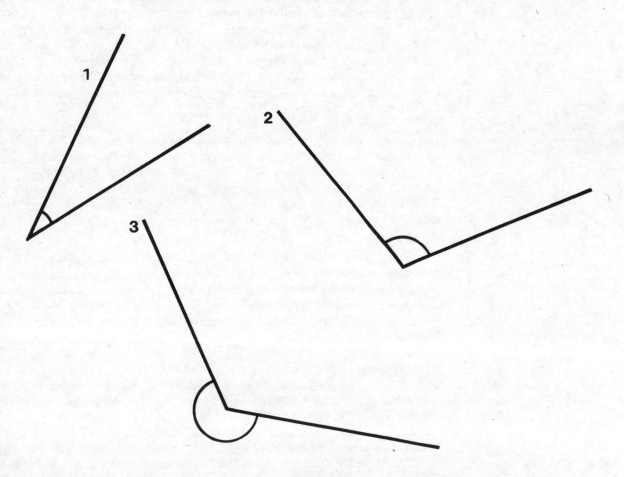

Figure 2.2

2.49 For each angle, estimates within a given range were coded as acceptable. The limits for these ranges were determined after discussion with testers. It should be noted that different tolerances were used for each angle as it was considered that the three angles were not equally difficult to estimate.

2.50 The first angle measured 33° and estimates between 25° and 40° were coded as acceptable. 46 per cent responded within this range, while almost 35 per cent gave 45° as their answer. Testers asked how estimates were obtained and three-quarters said they had compared the angle with 90° or 45°, whilst a small number used other suitable methods such as picturing a 30° set square. Around 15 per cent said they had guessed.

2.51 Angle 2 measured 106°, and 70 per cent gave acceptable estimates between 95° and 115°. More than 10 per cent estimated 120°, and nearly 15 per cent gave answers below 90°. More than 80 per cent referred to 90° when asked how they had estimated the angle, and the incidence of guessing fell to between 5 and 10 per cent.

2.52 The reflex angle presented difficulties for some pupils. The actual size was 235° and 42 per cent of pupils gave acceptable estimates between 210° and 260°. About 20 per cent gave responses in the range 91° to 140°, suggesting that they had considered the unlabelled part of the angle. The lower success rate for this question and an increase in omission rate to between 5 and 10 per cent suggest a lack of familiarity with reflex angles or their measurement. The most common successful method was to compare the angle with 180°, though others estimated the obtuse angle and subtracted from 360°.

2.53 Pupils were then asked to draw as best they could angles of 70° and 170° using only a ruler and pencil. 71 per cent drew the acute angle to within 10°, most using 90° as a reference. With the 170° angle, 62 per cent drew the angles in the range 160° to 179°, most pupils using 180° as a starting point. In attempting to draw the angle of 170°, over 5 per cent marked acute angles and 10 per cent indicated reflex angles, thus revealing uncertainty with large angles.

2.54 When asked what could be used to check the estimates of angles, more than 80 per cent suggested a protractor and over 5 per cent provided an appropriate description of one without being able to give the name. Examples of such descriptions are *"A half circle thing"*, *"An arc shape"*, *"One of those plastic things you put on top"*. A few suggested compasses while other unusual ideas were *"subtractor"*, *"projector"* and *"barometer"*.

2.55 Pupils were offered a choice of semi-circular or circular protractors or an angle indicator with which to measure the three angles in Figure 2.2. Initially, over 85 per cent opted for the conventional semi-circular protractor, some pupils expressing surprise that the others were in fact for measuring angles.

2.56 The success rates for angles 1 and 2 were both around 70 per cent. (Answers to within 1° were counted as acceptable.) With angle 1 (33°) nearly 10 per cent correctly positioned the protractor but misread the scale. Some of these merely used the wrong scale and gave an answer between 146° and 148°, while others failed to appreciate the direction of the scale and gave responses such as 47° or 153° (as can be seen from Figure 2.3).

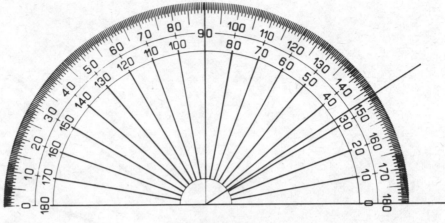

Figure 2.3

2.57 Similar errors were made with the obtuse angle of 106°: 5 per cent gave answers between 73° and 75° and a further 10 per cent made other errors in reading the scale.

2.58 Angle 3 (235°) was correctly measured by 41 per cent, with nearly 20 per cent changing to one of the 360° protractors. Approximately 15 per cent correctly used one of the circular protractors and a similar percentage measured the obtuse angle using the semi-circular protractor and subtracting from 360° to obtain the answer. The rest calculated the answer as 180° + 55° using the semi-circular protractor. Almost 25 per cent gave responses between 124° and 126°, the size of the unlabelled angle, and nearly 10 per cent did not attempt to measure the angle.

2.59 Pupils were then shown the triangle ABC (Figure 2.4) and asked to estimate the sizes of the angles.

2.60 The actual sizes were A = 45°, B = 115° and C = 20°. Estimates within 5° were judged acceptable for angle A, while margins of 10° were allowed for angles B and C. 28 per cent estimated all three angles within these ranges and a further 26 per cent gave two out of three acceptable estimates. When testers questioned pupils about the methods they used, over half replied that they had just estimated all three angles and about 30 per cent said they had estimated two angles and subtracted from 180° to get the remaining angle. A few pupils had estimated all three but then totalled the estimates and revised them in order to make the total 180°.

2.61 Pupils who did not use the angle sum of a triangle as part of their strategy were asked what the total should be and what their estimates totalled. When asked to revise their estimates so that they totalled 180°, a number of pupils did this in an unsystematic way, often making all the necessary adjustment on one angle.

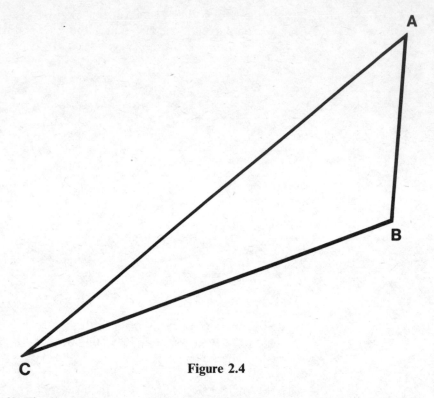

Figure 2.4

2.62 Finally pupils were asked to explain in words what an angle is. 4 per cent gave responses judged to be acceptable and examples of these are given below:

> *"The degree of turn between two intersecting lines."*
> *"Amount of rotation between two lines where they meet."*

2.63 Around 30 per cent defined an angle as the distance, area or space between two lines and examples of such responses are:

> *"Distance measured between two lines."*
> *"The gap in between where two lines meet."*
> *"Area between two lines."*
> *"The spacing between two lines which meet at a fixed point."*

These were not considered acceptable since no mention was made of how the space between the lines is measured. It can be seen from the written tests (see paragraphs 3.60 – 3.63) that some 20 per cent of pupils judged the size of angles on irrelevant features such as the size of the arc which labels the angle or the length of the bounding lines.

2.64 A further 10 per cent simply said an angle was where two lines meet and others said an angle was a corner. Nearly 10 per cent defined an angle in terms of degrees, for example:

> *"Number of degrees between two straight lines."*
> *"So many degrees, like a circle is 360°."*
> *"An amount of degrees."*

2.65 Almost one quarter did not respond to this question and many pupils were surprised at being asked to explain the concept of an angle. Indeed one pupil commented *"People talk about angles but do not mention what they are."*

Comparisons between boys and girls

2.66 Boys' success rates were generally higher than girls', although only on estimating the acute angle was the difference significant.

Table 2.3 *Results of the topic on angles**

	All %	Boys %	Girls %
1. Estimate the size of this angle (Figure 2.1, 90°)	85	89	81
2. Estimate the size of angle 1 (Figure 2.2, 33°, accept 25°–40°)	46	55	37
3. Estimate the size of angle 2 (Figure 2.2, 106°, accept 95°–115°)	70	72	67
4. Estimate the size of angle 3 (Figure 2.2, 235°, accept 210°–260°)	42	43	41
5. Using only a ruler and pencil, draw, as best you can, an angle of 70° (accept 60°–80°)	71	76	66
6. Draw, as best you can, an angle of 170° (accept 160°–179°)	62	65	59
7. What could you use to check your estimates?	82	82	81
8. Measure angle 1 (33°, accept + or −1°)	72	77	68
9. Measure angle 2 (106°, accept + or −1°)	69	72	65
10. Measure angle 3 (235°, accept + or −1°)	41	40	42
11. Estimate the sizes of the angles of this triangle ABC (Figure 2.4)	28	28	27
12. Can you tell me in words what an angle is?	4	5	3

*319 pupils took this topic.
The box indicates that the proportions within are significantly different statistically.

Comparisons with
primary topic

[1] *Mathematical
development. Primary
survey report No. 2.*
HMSO, 1981, price £5.80.

2.67 The angles topic which was given to 11 year old children was described in the second primary survey report[1]. Around 60 per cent of the primary pupils knew the term "right angle" and could give the number of degrees in it. This compares with 85 per cent of secondary pupils who estimated the angle in Figure 2.1 as 90°.

2.68 Since the primary pupils' performance in measuring angles differed considerably in 1978 and 1979 (see *the second primary survey report*), valid comparisons with success rates at secondary level can only be made for the first angle given to primary pupils. Around 40 per cent of primary pupils could measure an angle of 60°, compared with a 72 per cent success rate for an acute angle of 33° among secondary pupils.

Results of written items on angles are given in paragraphs 3.60 – 3.76 (see page 57).

Fractions

2.69 This topic tested pupils' understanding of the idea of a fraction and their concepts of basic operations with fractions.

2.70 Pupils were first asked to explain what was meant by a half of something and then to shade one half of a circle which was divided into 12 equal segments.

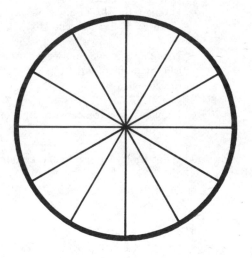

Figure 2.5

2.71 All pupils shaded the correct number of segments but many had difficulty in giving a precise definition of a half. 24 per cent gave an acceptable response; those who did not usually omitted to mention that the two parts should be equal: for example, they said that they were *"Split in two"* or *"Divided into two"*. After prompting many pupils realised that they had omitted this vital condition. A few could only explain what they meant by giving an example such as *"Half of 8 would be 4"*.

2.72 Pupils were then shown a diagram of a circle divided into 12 equal parts, 5 of which were shaded.

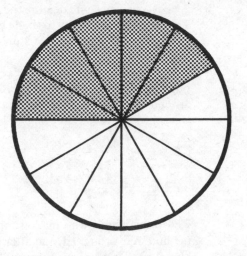

Figure 2.6

2.73 70 per cent were able to say what fraction of the circle was shaded, the most common wrong answer being $\frac{1}{2}$. A similar item in the written tests consisted of 13 squares, 5 of which were shaded and almost 80 per cent were able to give the fraction of the squares which was shaded.

2.74 When asked what was meant by two-thirds of something, 30 per cent gave an acceptable response. This higher success rate compared with the first question is probably due to the fact that pupils were prompted towards a better definition of a half and so appreciated what was required in this question. However, a quarter of the pupils still omitted to state that the parts should be equal and just over 10 per cent did not respond at all.

2.75 68 per cent correctly shaded in two-thirds of a circle divided into 12 equal segments (Figure 2.5). Generally pupils did this by working out that one-third of 12 is 4 and so two-thirds of the circle would be 8 segments. Some pupils just stated that $\frac{2}{3}$ was the same as $\frac{8}{12}$ or that 8 was $\frac{2}{3}$ of 12. A few estimated and shaded enough segments to "look like" $\frac{2}{3}$. The most frequent error was shading only 2 segments instead of two-thirds of the segments, thus illustrating $\frac{2}{12}$ or $\frac{1}{6}$.

2.76 The remaining questions in the topic tested pupils' competence in adding, multiplying and dividing fractions and their ability to represent these operations pictorially, again using circles divided into 12 equal segments (as in Figure 2.5).

2.77 Firstly, pupils were asked for the answer to $\frac{1}{2} + \frac{1}{4}$ and 72 per cent gave the correct response. 50 per cent did this mentally, explaining that $\frac{1}{2}$ was the same as $\frac{2}{4}$ and hence the answer was $\frac{3}{4}$. Around 10 per cent said they just knew the answer and a similar proportion got the correct response by working it out on paper. The most common mistake was to add numerators and denominators to give $\frac{2}{6}$, which some then cancelled to $\frac{1}{3}$. Around 10 per cent did this and slightly less added denominators only to give $\frac{1}{6}$.

2.78 84 per cent could demonstrate on the circles how to find the answer to $\frac{1}{2} + \frac{1}{4}$. The method was usually to shade both $\frac{1}{2}$ and $\frac{1}{4}$ on the same circle, although 10 per cent correctly demonstrated how to get the answer using 2 circles.

2.79 In the next question 47 per cent gave the correct answer to $\frac{3}{4} + \frac{2}{3}$, with some pupils leaving the answer as $1\frac{7}{12}$. 10 per cent could not answer this question, and around 15 per cent added numerators and denominators to give $\frac{5}{7}$. A few pupils 'cancelled' before attempting to add:

$$\overset{1}{\cancel{3}}{\Large/}_{4} \;+\; \frac{2}{\underset{1}{\cancel{3}}} \quad \text{or} \quad \frac{3}{\underset{2}{\cancel{4}}} \;+\; \overset{1}{\cancel{2}}{\Large/}_{3} \quad \text{or both.}$$

2.80 Some pupils who made simple errors in using the common denominator method were prompted, and after this help the success rate increased to just over half. A similar proportion were able to demonstrate how to get the answer on the circles.

2.81 The performance of primary pupils in adding fractions was analysed in some detail in the second primary survey report. In the written tests almost 60 per cent of primary pupils got $\frac{1}{2} + \frac{1}{4}$ correct while 13 per cent added numerators and denominators. More complex questions had facilities around 35 per cent, with about 20 per cent adding numerators and denominators. Thus, although success rates at the secondary level were around 10–15 per cent higher than among primary pupils, the strategy of adding numerators and denominators was almost as widely used by 15 year olds as with 11 year olds.

2.82 Division of fractions proved to be the most difficult operation, with a 40 per cent success rate for the question $\frac{1}{3} \div 2$. A quarter of the pupils used the 'turn upside down and multiply' algorithm while the rest just stated that a half of $\frac{1}{3}$ was $\frac{1}{6}$. More than 25 per cent of pupils did not attempt this question, while others showed that they had some knowledge of the algorithm but were not clear how to apply it. In the written tests 48 per cent were able to solve $\frac{1}{2} \div 2$.

2.83 43 per cent demonstrated the division on the circles by shading 4 sections to give $\frac{1}{3}$, then indicating half of those 4 sections to give $\frac{2}{12}$ or $\frac{1}{6}$.

2.84 Finally pupils were asked to work out $\frac{3}{4} \times \frac{1}{3}$ and 53 per cent correctly did this. A number of pupils just multiplied numerators and denominators and left the answer as $\frac{3}{12}$. Nearly 15 per cent found a common denominator for the fractions, again revealing confusion between the rules for addition and multiplication of fractions. In the written tests, just over half the pupils obtained the correct answer to a similar question, $\frac{1}{4} \times \frac{2}{3}$.

2.85 In order to demonstrate the multiplication on the circles it is necessary to replace the "multiply" by "of" or to interpret multiplying by $\frac{1}{3}$ as dividing by 3. The question is also made easier by reversing the order of the fractions. The task proved difficult for many pupils and only 24 per cent were successful.

2.86 Testers commented that very few pupils seemed familiar with a pictorial representation of operations with fractions. It was felt that many pupils learned during the topic. Indeed several pupils themselves commented on this with remarks such as *"I've never looked at it like that before"*. Another point made by the testers was that while some pupils successfully used the diagrams and were then able to correct their faulty use of an algorithm, many others did not query any discrepancy between the written and pictorial answers.

Comparisons between boys and girls

2.87 There was no pattern in the differences between boys and girls in this topic.

Table 2.4 *Results of the topic on fractions**

	All %	Boys %	Girls %
1. What is meant by half of something?	24	21	26
2. Shade in half of this circle	100	100	100
3. What fraction of the circle is shaded? $(\frac{5}{12})$	70	70	71
4. What is meant by two-thirds of something?	30	30	30
5. Shade in two-thirds of this circle	68	73	62
6. What is the answer to this? $(\frac{1}{2} + \frac{1}{4})$	72	78	65
7. Demonstrate using the circles	84	87	81
8. What is the answer to this? $(\frac{3}{4} + \frac{2}{3})$	47	44	51
9. Demonstrate using the circles	52	53	51
10. What is the answer to this? $(\frac{1}{3} \div 2)$	40	40	40
11. Demonstrate using the circles	43	46	40
12. What is the answer to this? $(\frac{3}{4} \times \frac{1}{3})$	53	47	60
13. Demonstrate using the circles	24	22	27

*326 pupils took this topic.
The box indicates that the proportions within are significantly different statistically.

Visualisation

2.88 This topic tested pupils' ability to construct three-dimensional models from two-dimensional projections. Pupils were presented with a series of diagrams of models and asked to construct each one in turn, using a set of wooden cubes.

2.89 Nearly all pupils were able to make the model shown in Figure 2.7.

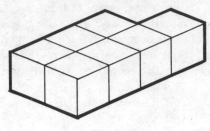

Figure 2.7

2.90 Pupils were then shown Figure 2.8 and asked to imagine the reflection of the shape in the mirror and construct the reflection with as few moves as possible.

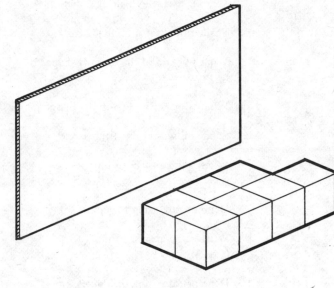

Figure 2.8

79 per cent did this by moving just one cube and a further 7 per cent did so by moving the row of three cubes.

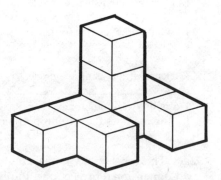

Figure 2.9

2.91 The model for Figure 2.9 was correctly made in almost all cases but constructing the reflection as indicated in Figure 2.10 presented some problems. (Note: the diagram given to pupils was not lettered.)

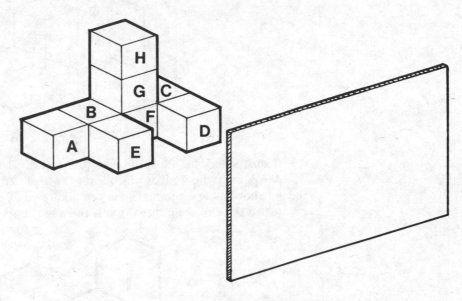

Figure 2.10

2.92 57 per cent obtained the correct shape by moving cubes D and E to the opposite side, while 14 per cent succeeded by moving the column FGH in between D and E and then moving A alongside E.

2.93 All pupils could say how many cubes would be needed to make the shape in Figure 2.11 and all succeeded in making it.

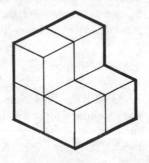

Figure 2.11

2.94 Pupils were then asked where a mirror could be placed so that the reflection could be made without moving any of the cubes. 28 per cent of pupils indicated two or three suitable positions for the mirror and a further 23 per cent pointed to one correct position. The most common errors were to place the mirror at the back or front of the shape or above it, parallel to the table.

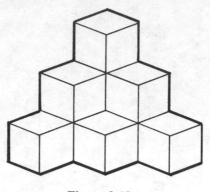

Figure 2.12

2.95 Constructing the model in Figure 2.12 caused few problems and when asked to point to those cubes which had to be used to make the model but which did not show in the diagram, 64 per cent indicated all four. Around 20 per cent pointed to three of them, usually just the three cubes in the bottom layer.

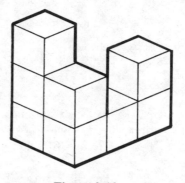

Figure 2.13

2.96 The success rate for constructing the model in Figure 2.13 was again over 90 per cent. Pupils were then asked to indicate the space where a cube could be placed that would not show in the diagram and 80 per cent did this correctly.

Comparisons between boys and girls
Comparisons between primary and secondary

2.97 The results were similar for boys and girls on all questions.

2.98 With the exception of the questions on constructing reflections of models, the secondary topic was largely the same as the primary version which has been fully reported in *Primary survey reports Nos. 1* and *2*. Constructing the simple models in Figures 2.7, 2.9 and 2.11 was done equally well by the two age groups.

2.99 Only Figures 2.12 and 2.13 produced an increased success rate at the secondary level.

2.100 Around 70 per cent of 11 year olds could make the model in Figure 2.12 but of the 15 year olds almost 95 per cent were successful. However, the question asking which cubes in the model did not show in the diagram produced an increase in success rate of around only 10 per cent between the two age levels.

2.101 Constructing the model in Figure 2.13 was done successfully by about 10 per cent more secondary pupils than primary pupils, but when asked where a cube could be placed which would not show in the picture, around 20 per cent more secondary pupils answered correctly.

Table 2.5 *Results of the topic on visulisation**

	All %	Boys %	Girls %
1. Make the model in Figure 2.7	98	100	97
2. Make the reflection with as few moves as possible (Figure 2.8)	79	82	77
3. Make the model in Figure 2.9	98	97	98
4. Make the reflection with as few moves as possible (Figure 2.10)	57	56	59
5. How many cubes are needed to make this shape? (Figure 2.11)	100	99	100
5a. Make it	100	100	99
5b. Where could you put a mirror so that the reflection is the same?	28	27	29
6. Make the model in Figure 2.12	93	97	90
6a. Which cubes do not show in the diagram?	64	69	61
7. Make the model in Figure 2.13	92	91	93
7a. Where could you put a cube which doesn't show in the picture?	80	80	79

*308 pupils took this topic.

Calculators

2.102 The 1978 version of this topic, as described in the first secondary survey report, was modified for the 1979 survey. The purpose of the questions remained the same, namely to assess pupils' ability to use the calculator, to use appropriate techniques such as approximating or using inverse operations for checking answers, and to recognise the importance of the order of operations. An account is given below of the results obtained in 1979.

2.103 90 per cent of the pupils said they had used a calculator before, mostly at home for checking homework, working out bills or doing puzzles, although around 30 per cent said they had used calculators at school.

2.104 No problems were experienced with the practice questions given before the test proper. Virtually all pupils successfully used the calculator to find the answers to straightforward multiplication and subtraction questions given at the beginning of the topic. 81 per cent obtained the correct answer to $\dfrac{17.6 \times 154.3}{10.9}$.

2.105 46 per cent of the pupils could approximate 57.6 × 13 within the range 600–900, the actual answer being 748.8. Pupils were permitted to use pencil and paper to get their approximation. Over 20 per cent were unable to estimate the answer. The method adopted by almost 15 per cent to get their approximation was to round 57.6 to 60 and then work out either 60 × 13 or 60 × 10. Others did 57 × 10 and then added a notional amount to compensate for the rounding. Some methods revealed that the distribution of addition over multiplication was not understood:

> "50 × 10 is 500 and 7 × 3 is 21, so answer is 521"
> "Times by 10 to give 576 so × by 13 gives 576.3".

2.106 Half the pupils could suggest the inverse operation which would check the answer to a subtraction question. The inverse operations needed to check $\dfrac{17.6 \times 154.3}{10.9}$ proved more difficult and 27 per cent were able to give the correct sequence of multiplying by 10.9 and then dividing by 17.6 or 154.3 to expect 154.3 or 17.6 respectively. A further 5 per cent described other suitable methods such as multiplying their answer by 10.9 and checking whether the result was the same as the answer to 17.6 × 154.3.

2.107 The last section of the topic tested pupils' understanding of algebraic notation as well as the importance of the order of operations. Firstly pupils were asked to give an approximate value for v, given the relationship $v = u + gt$ and values $u = 73.1$, $g = 9.8$ and $t = 7.5$. The actual value for v was 146.6 and 30 per cent gave estimates between 140 and 150, while nearly 35 per cent added the three values together. When asked to work out the answer on the calculator, 51 per cent were successful. 15 per cent entered the variables into the calculator in the order 73.1 + 9.8 × 7.5 and hence evaluated $(u + g) \times t$. Around 20 per cent of pupils added these three numbers together. This proportion was smaller than in the case of the estimation task, probably because some pupils had realised their error and others had been told that gt meant $g \times t$.

2.108 In the final question pupils were asked for the value of v, given the same formula, rearranged as $v = gt + u$. Most pupils said that the answer would be the same, although some failed to appreciate the commutative property of addition and worked out the value using the calculator.

Comparisons between boys and girls

2.109 There were no differences in performance in using the calculator. The only significant difference was in estimating the answer to 57.6 × 13 where nearly 60 per cent of the boys were within the acceptable range compared with just over 30 per cent of the girls.

Sheets of calculations presented to pupils

1. 57.6 × 13
2. 95.78 − 7.9
3. $\dfrac{17.6 \times 154.3}{10.9}$
4. $v = u + gt$, $u = 73.1$, $g = 9.8$, $t = 7.5$
5. $v = gt + u$ with same values for u, g and t.

Table 2.6   *Results of the topic on calculators**

	All %	Boys %	Girls %
1a. Approximately what is the answer to number 1? (Responses between 600 and 900 coded as correct)	46	58	32
1b. Now work it out using the calculator. (Answer 748.8)	98	97	98
2a. Use the calculator to find the answer to number 2 (Answer 87.88)	99	98	100
2b. How could you check this using the calculator?	50	48	51
3a. Use the calculator to find the answer to number 3 (Answer 249.14495)	81	80	81
3b. How could you check this using the calculator?	32	36	27
4a. Approximately what is the value of v when u, g and t take these values? (Sheet 4 presented, responses between 140 and 150 coded as correct)	30	33	26
4b. Now work it out using the calculator	51	53	48
5. What is the value of v here? (Sheet 5 presented) no working	51	54	46
with calculator	8	7	9

*329 pupils took this topic.
The box indicates that the proportions within are significantly different statistically.

Length

2.110 This topic was largely the same as the 1978 version which was described in the first secondary survey report. Pupils were required to give definitions of mathematical terms and then estimate and measure the lengths of both straight and curved lines.

2.111 It was clear that while many pupils were familiar with the words "perimeter", "circumference" and "diameter", they were unable to give precise definitions of them. Around 15 per cent simply said the perimeter of a rectangle was "the outside" without any mention of length, while other descriptions revealed confusion between perimeter and area. Indeed one pupil said perimeter was *"just a posh name for area"*. 69 per cent gave suitable descriptions of the circumference of a circle, whereas 48 per cent could provide a satisfactory definition of diameter. About 15 per cent said the diameter was "a line across the circle" without mentioning that the line should go through the centre. Some pupils introduced other circle terms into their definitions, for example, several pupils described the diameter as *"the largest chord in a circle"*, while one said it was *"the distance between two parallel tangents"*.

2.112 Pupils were asked to estimate and measure the lengths of a straight line and the perimeter of a rectangle.

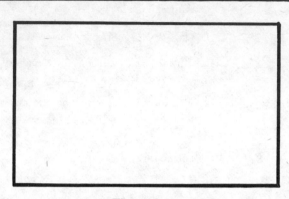

Figure 2.14

2.113 The actual length of the line was 7.7 cm and 68 per cent gave acceptable estimates. It had been agreed with testers that responses between 6 and 9 cm or between 2.5 and 3.5 inches should be coded as correct. 58 per cent measured the line accurately. One side of the ruler was graduated in centimetres and millimetres while the other side had only centimetres marked. Some pupils were unable to read the mm scale correctly and gave responses such as *"7½ and a little bit"*, "3 away from 8 cm". Others used the side of ruler graduated in cm only and could respond only with answers such as *"nearly 8 cm"*, *"7¾ cm"* or *"just over 7½ cm"*. 66 per cent gave estimates of the perimeter of the rectangle between 18 and 28 cm or between 7 and 11 inches and 75 per cent were able to measure the length to within 4 mm, the actual distance being 22.6 cm.

2.114 The final set of questions was concerned with the circumference of a circle.

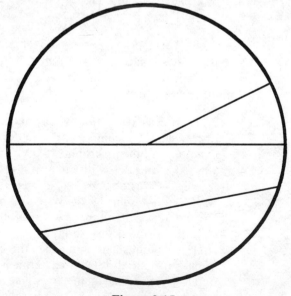

Figure 2.15

2.115 When asked to estimate the length of the circumference of the circle shown in Figure 2.15, 51 per cent of pupils gave estimates within the range 17 to 27 cm, the actual length being 22 cm. 66 per cent were able to use string to measure the circumference to within 1 cm, while 36 per cent successfully used the formula $C = \pi D$. Most of the pupils who had obtained two answers for the length of the circumference considered that using the formula was the more accurate method. The reason generally given was that fitting the string was imprecise although some added that π was exact. Others said that the formula only involved measuring a straight line which was more reliable than using string.

Comparisons between boys and girls

2.116 Success rates for boys were higher than those for girls on all questions, although the only significant difference was in the task involving measurement of the length of the straight line.

Table 2.7   *Results of the topic on length**

	All %	Boys %	Girls %
1. Estimate the length of this line (Figure 2.14, actual length 7.7 cm, answers between 6 and 9 cm coded as correct)	68	69	66
2. Estimate the perimeter of this rectangle (Figure 2.14, actual length 22.6 cm, answers between 18 and 28 cm coded as correct)	66	69	62
3. Check your estimate of the line by measuring (Answer 7.7 cm)	58	65	51
4. Check your estimate of the perimeter (Answers between 22.2 and 23 cm coded as correct)	75	78	72
5. What is the circumference of a circle?	69	71	67
6. What is the diameter of a circle?	48	51	45
7. Show me the circumference of this circle (Figure 2.15 presented)	83	87	80
8. Show me the diameter drawn on this circle (Figure 2.15)	84	88	81
9. Estimate the length of the circumference of this circle (Figure 2.15, actual length 22 cm, answers between 17 and 27 cm coded as correct)	51	56	45

10. Check your estimate
  (i) String (answers to within 1 cm coded as correct)
  (ii) $C = \pi D$
	66
	36
		68
		40
			64
			32

*333 pupils took this topic.
The box indicates that the proportions within are significantly different statistically.

Mass

2.117 This topic was largely the same as the 1978 version which was described in detail in the first secondary survey report.

2.118 Using only a balance, 91 per cent of pupils successfully found the heaviest of five wooden blocks which were identical in appearance. Pupils were then asked to place the blocks in order from heaviest to lightest and 62 per cent obtained the correct order. The most popular method of tackling this question, used by almost 55 per cent, was to set aside the block already identified as the heaviest, find the heaviest of the remaining four and then continue the process until the order had been established. Nearly 10 per cent compared the heaviest block with each of the others and based their response on how far down the balance tipped each time.

2.119 Pupils were then presented with a 20 g mass and asked whether they called it a 'mass' or 'weight'. 14 per cent said they used the word 'mass' and the rest referred to it as a 'weight'. Whichever word they chose was used in the remaining questions.

2.120 93 per cent were able to make a lump of plasticine as heavy as a 20 g mass. When asked to make a lump of plasticine a quarter as heavy as the 20 g mass, 31 per cent of the pupils correctly used two weighings to find a half of a half of the 20 g piece. 32 per cent divided the plasticine by eye without using the balance, while 22 per cent were unable to start the task. Where necessary pupils were prompted to use the balance and those unable to start were told to first make a lump weighing half of 20 g. After these prompts, the success rate rose to 80 per cent.

2.121 The final section of the topic was concerned with finding the mass of a peg using the balance and the 20 g mass. About a third of the pupils were able to explain the method of counting how many pegs weighed 20 g and then dividing 20 by the number of pegs. A further 5 per cent described suitable methods involving the use of a 5 g piece of plasticine made in an earlier section of the topic. When asked to carry out the task, 45 per cent were successful.

2.122 About 42 pegs weighed 20 g and a number of pupils had difficulties with the arithmetic involved. Just over 15 per cent were able to calculate the answer as a decimal and about the same number stated that a peg weighed "about $\frac{1}{2}$ g". Around 10 per cent wrote the answer as a fraction, e.g. $\frac{20}{42}$ and some of these pupils then cancelled the fraction to its lowest terms.

Comparisons between boys and girls

2.123 About 20 per cent of the boys said they used the word 'mass', compared with under 10 per cent of the girls. 39 per cent of the boys successfully quartered the 20 g lump of plasticine compared with 22 per cent of the girls, the difference being significant. 45 per cent of the girls quartered the plasticine without using the balance whereas only 20 per cent of the boys used this method.

2.124 The results of other sections of the topic did not show any differences between boys and girls.

Table 2.8   *Results of the topic on mass**

		All %	Boys %	Girls %
1. Use the balance to find out which of these blocks is the heaviest		91	92	89
2. Place the blocks in order, from heaviest to lightest		62	61	63
3. Present 20 g mass. Do you call this a 20 g mass or a 20 g weight?	Mass	14	19	7
	Weight	85	79	91
	Either	1	1	1
4. Make a lump of plasticine that is as heavy as this 20 g mass/weight		93	96	90
5. Make a lump of plasticine that is a quarter as heavy as this 20 g mass/weight		31	39	22
6. How would you find the mass/weight of one of these pegs using this apparatus?		37	40	33
7. Do it		45	46	43

*332 pupils took this topic.
The box indicates that the results within are significantly different statistically.

Pinboard triangles, 1978 topic only

2.125 A central feature of this topic was the use of a pinboard (or geoboard), a piece of equipment consisting of nails arranged in a square matrix which is often used in schools to develop a range of ideas in space and number.

2.126 In this instance the task which the pupils were set was a fairly common exercise: to make as many different triangles as possible using an elastic band on a board with 9 nails. When each triangle had been constructed it was drawn on paper which had sets of 9 dots printed on it corresponding to the 9 points of the pinboard. Pupils then had a record of triangles already made and were therefore able to explore new variations of shape on a pinboard uncluttered with previous constructions.

2.127 The purpose of the task was to establish how many different triangles pupils could make and to note whether they employed a systematic approach to obtaining them. The ability to draw the triangle was not being tested and so the tester assisted if pupils had difficulties in copying it.

2.128 Initially the pupil was presented with the pinboard and asked to make one triangle with an elastic band. When this was completed the dotted paper was produced and the pupil requested to draw the shape on it. Any error made in copying was pointed out and the pupil was asked to try again. If an error was made again the tester drew the correct shape, and the testers were instructed to do the drawing themselves if errors were continually made by the pupil. No instances of this being necessary during the survey were reported by testers, although there had been one such case during the pilot stage.

2.129 It is possible to make eight triangles of different sizes or shapes on the board. The first triangles made by about 90 per cent of the pupils was one of only 3 of the possible 8 triangles. Nearly half of those who took the topic first made a triangle which utilised 3 neighbouring pins. For example:

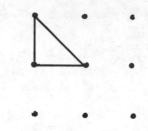

2.130 Nearly all the remainder drew one of the following two types of triangle (in nearly equal proportions):

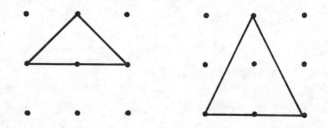

2.131 Pupils were given the opportunity to make as many triangles as they wished before any cases of congruent shapes were drawn to their attention and the meaning, in this context, of the term 'different' established. Some pupils themselves asked what was counted as 'different' or commented, without prompting, that one they had just drawn was the same as a previous one.

2.132 About a quarter did not produce congruent triangles. Nearly all pupils who did were able to say in what respects they were different. A few referred appropriately to one being a rotation or a reflection or a translation of the other. Most said the triangles were in different directions or positions. Less sophisticated but sufficiently descriptive responses were:

> "Same but upside down."
> "Same but moved over."
> "The corners are facing different directions."

2.133 A few phrased their explanations in an insufficiently general manner:

> "It's the other way round."
> "One is the right way up, the other is going the other way."

2.134 Few pupils gave evidence of using any system in their search for triangles, but testers were not asked to question pupils about how they had set about the task. A common strategy which was noted consisted of fixing one line and moving one point of the elastic band to various positions but it was not always clear from testers' accounts whether pupils had been completely methodical. Examples of testers' recording of this strategy were:

> Fixed two points, moved one. Moved board around to compare ones already done.

> Initially kept diagonal constant and moved third point, but then moved on to random discovery.

Another strategy was:

> Dealt with top 6 dots first. Kept one side horizontal.

Also noted:

> Examined drawings to find out how he could alter triangles.

> Removed band each time and studied blank board.

2.135 About a quarter of the pupils ultimately found all 8 triangles. This included those pupils who did so after being asked if they could make some more. The triangle which testers reported was most elusive was:

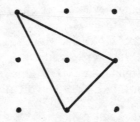

This may be because pupils tend to see triangles as having a horizontal base; in fact the term 'base' itself suggests this.

2.136 Testers' evaluations of this topic were extremely varied and ranged all the way from *"A good test for everyone"* and *"One of the more popular topics, particularly with those who employed a sensible strategy"* to *"It was the least satisfactory of all the tests"*. The main weakness was perhaps that the presentation did not suggest to many pupils that the use of some systematic strategy would be helpful.

Correlations: practical topics and written tests

Relationships between 1979 practical survey topics

2.137 Each practical test consisted of three topics. In order to gain some idea of the consistency with which pupils performed on the three topics in the test they were given, topic scores were correlated. The topic scores were computed by giving one mark for unaided correct responses to each question in the topic and then summing a pupil's marks for the topic. Where only an answer or a method was required in response to a question, then the mark was given for a correct answer or a correct method. The responses to some questions were coded for both answer and method, and, in these cases, a half mark was given for a correct response to each.

2.138 The design of the practical mathematics survey (see Table 2.2) only permitted each topic to be correlated with six other topics. Each correlation was based on the scores of about 100 pupils.

2.139 All of the correlations obtained were significant at the 5 per cent level and 22 of the 30 correlations were significant at the 0.1 per cent level. The topic on visualisation had the lowest correlations with other topics, probably due to the restricted range of scores it produced. The topic on area had the next lowest correlations.

Relationship between written test results and practical topics

2.140 The pupils who took a practical test were a sub-sample of those who took a written test.

2.141 Each written test consisted of questions from three different sub-categories and scores for these were computed by awarding one mark for every question answered correctly. Each pupil then had 3 practical topic scores and 3 written test sub-category scores. These scores were correlated and a 15 (sub-categories) $\times$ 10 (topics) matrix of correlations resulted. Each correlation was based on the scores of about 60 pupils who answered questions on a given sub-category and a given practical topic.

2.142 Nearly two-thirds of these correlations were above 0.50 and all but 7 of them were significantly different from zero statistically. Five of these non-significant correlations involved the topic on visualisation and the other two involved the topic on area.

2.143 The topics most highly correlated with the written test scores were fractions, calculators, length and angles. Correlations of over 0.75 were obtained between the number skills sub-category and the length, fractions and calculators practical topics.

Summary

Testers' reports

2.144 The testers reported that they were well received in almost all schools and that suitable accommodation was nearly always provided. Many testers commented that they found the survey an enjoyable and valuable experience and that they welcomed the opportunity to talk about mathematics with a variety of pupils.

2.145 After the survey, testers were asked to write comments on each topic and on the practical testing in general. These have proved to be invaluable in improving existing topics and developing new ones. In addition, testers attended a one-day meeting in January 1980 at which particular issues were discussed and ideas exchanged.

2.146 Comments on the suitability of the tests were generally favourable, for example: "I found the tests provided a challenge for all abilities, without leaving the least able feeling totally inadequate". Several remarked that they thought that some less able pupils performed better than might be expected, for example:

"Many of the less academic pupils were able to solve practical problems while the more able did not always understand the practical aspect". It is intended to explore these relationships more fully in the data.

2.147 A number of testers commented on the difficulties pupils had in giving explanations, for example: "Many children were able to write down or perform an operation which they could not explain in words". Some considered that this pointed to a lack of discussion of work in mathematics classrooms. Although language presented problems to some pupils, the practical mode allowed pupils to demonstrate their intuitive ideas without being hindered by reading problems.

The results

2.148 In the topic on probability, two-thirds of the pupils could predict the most likely outcomes of a number of tosses of a coin and throws of a single die. Over half believed that the outcomes of throwing two dice were equally likely. The explanations given for predictions before an experiment was conducted, or for the results afterwards, were often given in terms of pupils' previous experiences.

2.149 Around 70 per cent were able to use a protractor to measure an acute and an obtuse angle and about 40 per cent could do so in the case of a reflex angle. Pupils' accuracy in estimating angle size varied with the task: over 60 per cent drew, acceptably, an acute and an obtuse angle of given sizes. 4 per cent of the pupils gave an acceptable explanation of what an angle is, about 30 per cent defining it as the distance, area or space between two lines.

2.150 Circles divided into 12 equal sectors were used to explore pupils' understanding of fractions and fraction calculations. About 70 per cent gave correct responses to questions on the fractions which were represented by shaded sectors. Over 80 per cent could demonstrate $\frac{1}{2} + \frac{1}{4}$ on the circles whilst 50 per cent could do this for $\frac{3}{4} + \frac{2}{3}$. 15 per cent added numerators and denominators when asked to add fractions before using the circles.

2.151 The topic on visualisation tested pupils' performance in interpreting two-dimensional diagrams of three-dimensional models. Over 90 per cent successfully constructed the models with cubes, given pictures of them. Fewer, though still a high proportion of pupils, could also answer questions about the positions of cubes which were not visible in the picture. Problems of varying difficulty involving reflections of the models were also given to the pupils.

2.152 Of those who took the Calculators topic, 90 per cent had claimed to have used one before. Virtually all could do a single operation computation correctly and 80 per cent could do a two-operation calculation. The proportions of pupils who could check their results, by using inverse operations, for example, were 50 per cent fewer than the proportions who could calculate correctly.

2.153 The length and mass topics were largely the same as in 1978. About 70 per cent could use a ruler and about 90 per cent a balance to carry out basic measurement tasks. These proportions reflect performance in general on the measurement and other practical tasks in this mode of assessment. Pupils' understanding and communication of ideas were scored lower than this.

3 The written tests: item clusters

The 1979 survey: written tests

[1] *Mathematical development. Secondary survey report No. 1* HMSO, 1980, price £6.60.

3.1 Apart from a few items the written tests used for the 1979 secondary survey were the same as the tests which had been used in 1978. A brief account of the test design will be given here, but a full account of the development of the tests and the test design can be found in the report on the first secondary mathematics survey[1].

3.2 The 15 sub-categories assessed in the survey are listed in Table 3.1 together with the number of items used in each.

Table 3.1 *Number of items used within each sub-category in 1979 secondary survey.*

Main content category	Sub-category	Number of items
Number	Concepts	43
	Skills	53
	Applications	41
Measures	Unit	44
	Rate and ratio	21
	Mensuration	42
Algebra	General algebra	42
	Traditional algebra	50
	Modern algebra	44
	Graphical algebra	43
Geometry	Descriptive geometry	46
	Modern geometry	40
	Trigonometry	43
Probability and statistics	Probability	16
	Statistics	23

3.3 Each test contained items from three of the sub-categories, at least one of which was likely to be familiar to all of the pupils (i.e. any number or measures sub-category, general algebra, descriptive geometry.) The tests were divided into two clearly defined sections – a multiple choice section and a section where the pupil supplied the answer – and within these sections items were grouped together by sub-category and in approximate order of increasing difficulty within sub-category. The sub-categories were placed in the same order in the two parts and the five or so different parts of each sub-category were placed in the three different positions in the test as equally as possible. Table 3.2 shows the sub-categories appearing in each test.

3.4 In all, 12,459 tests were analysed, giving an effective sample size of approximately 1,650 pupils per sub-category once the data had been edited and weighted to provide representative proportions of pupils in each stratum of the sampling design. (See Appendix 1 for an account of the sample.)

Item clusters

3.5 The general picture of performance provided by the individual items in 1979 is much the same as that described in the first secondary survey. This chapter is therefore concerned with more detailed analyses of some clusters of items, a cluster consisting of items of related content. The analyses which follow highlight the facilities (success rates), rates of omission and the incidences of the more common errors made when the items are attempted. The differences in these proportions are then related to the differences in the items' content and context in order to attempt to identify the features associated with item difficulty.

3.6 The proportions of the sample responding in each type of response category (facility, error incidence, other uncoded responses, omission rate) are defined in terms of the ratio of the number of pupils making a particular response to the number who took a test which included the item. The ratios obtained are expressed as percentages.

3.7 Nearly all the items appeared in more than one test; the percentages given below are the means for these test appearances. Responses counted as correct are starred (*). Illustrative items are numbered consecutively through this chapter and each number is followed by a letter in brackets which is the code letter of the sub-category to which the item belongs. A list of sub-category code letters is given in Table 3.2.

Analyses of item clusters

Numeration

3.8 Numeration is concerned with the recording and reading of numbers. Obviously some understanding of numeration is involved in every type of numerical item but those aspects relating to the idea of place value are tested with specific kinds of item. These include questions about the value of digits in whole numbers and about the relative sizes of sets of numbers.

1(F) What is the value of the figure 7 in 1728?	Response	Given by
	*700	62%
	*Hundreds	8%
	100 or hundred	6%
	7	1%
	Others	13%
	Omitted	10%

3.9 In response to a request for the value of the figure in the hundreds column of 1728 (Item 1(F)) 62 per cent of the pupils gave the answer 700 and a further 8 per cent wrote "hundreds". The responses "100" or "hundred" were given by a further 6 per cent of the pupils but were not counted as correct, although the fault may lie more in the imprecision of the language used than in the understanding of place value. If this 6 per cent are given the benefit of the doubt then about three quarters of the pupils provided evidence, in their responses to 1(F), that they knew the place value of figures for at least the first two or three whole number places. A similar proportion selected the correct alternative in the item 2(F).

2(F) In which of the following does the 7 represent 7 'tens'?	Response	Given by
	107	3%
107	*71	75%
71	7	9%
7	710	11%
710	Others	0%
	Omitted	2%

3.10 Items 1(F) and 2(F) directly ask questions about place value, using terms such as 'value' and 'represent'. Item 3(F) was a more indirect means of testing pupils' knowledge of place value without using this terminology and some 80 per cent answered correctly. Moreover, it was omitted by only 2 per cent of the pupils in contrast to the 10 per cent who gave no response to 1(F). Item 2(F) also had a low rate of omission but is a multiple choice item – a format which tends to produce lower omission rates than that requiring pupils to supply their own responses.

Table 3.2 *Summary of test design showing the sub-categories covered in each test*

		Test No.	01	02	03	04	05	06	07
Number	F	Number Concepts	F1					F2	
	H	Number Skills		H1					H2
	J	Number Applications			J1			J2	
Measures	R	Measures Unit					R1		
	K	Measures Rate and ratio					K1		
	Q	Measures Mensuration			Q1				
Algebra	M	Algebra General	M1			M2			
	U	Algebra Traditional			U1				U2
	N	Algebra Modern			N1				N2
	V	Algebra Graphs				V1			
Geometry	P	Geometry Descriptive						P1	
	B	Geometry Modern	B1						
	S	Geometry Trigonometry					S1		
Probability and Statistics	W	Probability					W1		
	X	Statistics			X1				

3(F) Seven 'hundreds', twelve 'tens', and five 'ones' added together make	Responses	Given by
	*825 or 8 hundred and twenty five	80%
	717	2%
	7125	<1%
	Others	15%
	Omitted	2%

3.11 A comparison of the 15 year old pupils' responses to 2(F) and 3(F) with those of 11 year old pupils to similar items in the primary surveys provides additional evidence that the older pupils are not used to being directly asked about place value. For example, in response to the item 4, which was given to the 11 year old pupils and which corresponds to 1(F) from the secondary survey, 92 per cent selected the correct alternative.

4 (Primary)

Put a ring around the number which is the same as 7 tens.

Response	Selected by
107	1%
*70	92%
7	2%
710	3%
	Omitted by
	2%

08	09	10	11	12	13	14	15	16	17	18	19	20	21	22	23	24	25
					F3				F4				F5				
					H3		H4			H5					H6		
				J3				J4						J5			
R2				R3					R4							R5	
	K2						K3			K4							K5
Q2						Q3				Q4				Q5			
		M3					M4					M5					
		U3			U4				U5					U6			
			N3				N4					N5					
			V2						V3	V4						V5	
				P2		P3						P4					P5
B2						B3							B4			B5	
	S2							S3					S4				S5
	W2													W3			
		X2		X3						X4						X5	

3.12 Item 4 differs from 1(F) in details of presentation including the terms used ("same as" instead of "represents"). Most importantly, the correct alternative is 70 (a near equivalent of '7 tens') and not 71. In the 1980 primary survey the alternative 70 was replaced by 71 and the results for the two age groups can more validly be compared:

Response alternative	Selected by	
	Secondary	Primary
107	3%	2%
*71	75%	69%
7	9%	8%
710	11%	12%
Others	1%	6%
Omitted	3%	3%

3.13 The distribution of the selections of the younger pupils is very similar to that of the 15 year olds, showing that on this type of item the latter make little advance. It is notable that about the same proportion of 15 year olds as 11 year olds select 710 as their answer, presumably because of the zero in the units column.

3.14 However, the 15 year olds have made a greater advance in items such as 3(F) where place value is tested indirectly. About 60 per cent of primary pupils gave the correct answer to item 5 in contrast to the 80 per cent of 15 year olds who wrote the correct response to 3(F).

---

5 (Primary)

---

7 hundreds 5 tens and 12 units make ....

Nearly 20 per cent of the 11 year olds wrote a number which consisted of the given figures: 7512. This type of error accounted for the difference in facility between the age groups for it was rare among the 15 year olds.

3.15 Items relating to the relative sizes of sets of numbers had facilities which ranged from 80 per cent to over 90 per cent. The easiest of these items was 6(F), which had a facility of 93 per cent. However, over 90 per cent of 11 year olds could also do this item correctly. Fewer selected the correct response to 7(F), possibly because of the greater amount of information which pupils had to scan and also because a complete ordering of the given numbers had to be recognised, not just the largest number. Just over half of the 11 year olds could do items similar to 7(F).

6(F) Which of these numbers is the largest?	Selected by	
	15 year olds	11 year olds
A. 1998	3%	5%
*B. 2012	93%	91%
C. 2004	3%	2%
D. 897	<1%	2%
Omitted by	1%	0%

7(F) Which row of numbers is in order of size?

				Selected by
A. 275	752	725	575	4%
B. 752	572	725	527	7%
*C. 257	275	725	752	80%
D. 572	527	257	275	6%
			Omitted by	4%

3.16 The items 8(F) and 9(F) provided evidence of pupils' knowledge and understanding of decimal place value. 45 per cent gave acceptable answers to 8(F).

8(F) What is the value of the figure 1 in the decimal 2.31?

	Given by
*$\frac{1}{100}$ or 1 hundreth	36%
*.01	7%
hundredths	2%
1, unit, units	11%
0.1, $\frac{1}{10}$, 1 tenth or tenths	4%
Others	17%
Omitted	23%

3.17 The difference in facility between 8(F) and 9(F) may be due to the different ways in which the questions were put. Their facilities are some 30–40 per cent lower than those of 1(F) and 2(F) which relate to whole numbers only. In addition, the omission rate for 8(F) is 23 per cent compared with 10 per cent for 1(F), although both items are similar in format and in wording.

9(F) Write a fraction in the box to complete the statement

$$6.28 = (6 \times 1) + (2 \times \boxed{}) + (8 \times \tfrac{1}{100})$$

Response	Given by
*$\frac{1}{10}$	28%
*0.1 or .1	5%
$\frac{1}{100}$	2%
Others	37%
Omitted	28%

*Mathematical development. Primary survey report No. 2 HMSO. 1981. price £5.80.

3.18 Responses to the items 10(F) and 11(F), which required decimals to be compared, confirmed the discrepancy in the results obtained in 1978. That is, while 82 per cent selected the correct (largest) number in 10(F) only 34 per cent gave the correct alternative (the smallest number) in 11(F). The results for the whole number and the other decimal items suggest that the 80 per cent success rate for 10(F) is probably inflated by some pupils who may have selected the correct answer for spurious reasons – possibly because it is more obviously different from the other alternatives. Another factor that emerged when pupils were interviewed during the development of items, was that some of them associated the size of a decimal with the number of decimal places: the "longer" the decimal, the smaller the number and vice versa. This thinking appears to be related to the error made by some 11 year olds *(see the second primary survey* *report**) in response to items requiring the ordering of decimals, when pupils gave the largest number, when the smallest was asked for and vice versa. Thus 0.1 in 10(F) and 0.625 in 11(F) would be selected if these strategies were used, but whereas the former is the correct response to the item, the latter is not. These possibilities suggest that the "true" success rate for 10(F) – getting it right for the right reason – could be a good deal less than 80 per cent.

3.19 The incorrect alternative response to 10(F) which was chosen most frequently as the largest decimal, is in fact the largest number if the decimal points are ignored. In response to 11(F) 22 per cent chose the number which would have the smallest value if decimal points were ignored. In the primary survey it was found that about 25 per cent were probably ignoring decimal points in this type of item.

10(F) Which of the numbers below has the greatest value?	Selected by
A. 0.075	1–2%
B. 0.09	1–2%
*C. 0.1	82%
D. 0.089	14%
	Omitted by
	1–2%

11(F) Which of the numbers below has the smallest value?	Selected by
A. 0.625	34%
B. 0.25	3%
C. 0.375	2%
*D. 0.125	38%
E. 0.5	22%
	Omitted by
	1–2%

Adding and subtracting

3.20 Adding and subtracting numbers are among the most basic of mathematical operations. The items in this section all involve one or both these operations presented to the pupils in a variety of forms and contexts.

3.21 The highest facilities of about 90 per cent were obtained in response to straightforward items in algorithmic form where the numbers were presented vertically (12, 13 and 14). Neither the type of operation, addition in 12(H) and 13(H), subtraction in 14(H), nor the presence of decimal points in 13(H) affected the success rate differentially. In each case carrying or borrowing was required.

12(H)

```
    3 4 1
    7 5 3
  1 3 5 9
+     5 6
  _____

  _____
```

Response	Given by
2509*	90%
Others	9%
No response	<1%

13(H)

		Response	Given by
	0 . 3 1	3 4 . 6 9*	91%
	4 . 2 9	Others	9%
	6 . 0 3	No response	<1%
	1 2 . 4 1		
+1 1 . 6 5			

14(H)

	Response	Given by
4 9 8 1	3965*	90%
— 1 0 1 6	Others	9%
	No response	1%

15(H)

	Response	Given by
7 . 5 6	1.77*	82%
— 5 . 7 9	13.35	<2%
	Others	15%
	No response	<2%

3.22 15(H) is less straightforward, involving the subtraction of two decimal numbers with "borrowing" required in two consecutive columns. The facility is 8 per cent lower than that of 14(H). A small proportion (<2 per cent) added the two numbers instead of subtracting. The proportion who subtracted the lower from the higher number in the units and tens columns was not coded on this occasion and had any pupils used this tactic in the units column of 14(H) they could have obtained the correct units figure fortuituously.

3.23 The next group of four items 16, 17, 18 and 19(H) have lower facilities and higher omission rates than those already discussed. The principal difference between the two groups is that in this second group of four items the numbers were not presented vertically, so an understanding of place value is required as well as knowledge of addition and subtraction bonds.

16(H)
Add two hundred and three to one thousand and fifty.

	Response	Given by
	1253*	79%
	1253 (in words)	1%
Write your answer in figures	Others	18%
	No response	2%

17(H)

	Response	Given by
	9134*	83%
9417 — 283 = ...	Others	13%
	No response	5%

18(H)

	Response	Given by
	145.641*	69%
	8211	5%
$12.45 + 127.5 + 5.691 = \ldots\ldots$	(with or without decimal point)	
	Others	22%
	No response	4%

19(H)

	Response	Given by
	3.77*	64%
	494	6%
$5.07 - 1.3 = \ldots\ldots$	(with or without decimal point)	
	Others	21%
	No response	9%

3.24 Item 16(H) presents two numbers in words and no carrying is involved in the calculation which is made by the usual algorithmic procedure. 79 per cent gave the correct answer in figures, and a further 1 per cent provided it in words. A subtraction which involved borrowing in the tens column (17(H)) had a facility of 83 per cent.

3.25 Items 18 and 19(H) both involved calculating with numbers which had different numbers of decimal places and this feature produced a further decline to 69 per cent in the addition (item 18) and to 64 per cent in the case of subtraction (19). About 5 per cent gave responses to 18 and 19 which suggest that they had ignored place value as indicated by the decimal points and simply added (or subtracted) the given numbers. The proportion of those who made this error is smaller than the number who did so in response to items requiring the largest or smallest decimal numbers to be selected from alternatives (around 20 per cent, see paragraph 3.20).

3.26 The items in the numeration cluster differed from the ones discussed in this section in respect of the task (comparison or calculation), the numbers involved (all less than one in the comparison items) and the type of item (supply in the case of the items in this section and multiple choice in the comparison task). It is possible that the comparison task was made more difficult for those who do not understand decimal place value by the fact that in those cases all the numbers were less than one, whereas those in items 18 and 19 all had a whole number component.

20(H)

	Response	Given by
	4.34*	24%
$2.6 - 4.12 + 6.3 - 0.44 =$	7.38	11%
	Others	50%
	No response	15%

3.27 20(H) is a mixed operation item where the numbers are presented horizontally and decimals are involved. These features together reduced the success rate to 24 per cent and increased the proportion who omitted the item to 15 per cent. 11 per cent gave the answer 7.38 which can be obtained by wrongly subtracting 2.6 from 4.12 but then continuing the computation correctly.

*See *Children's understanding of mathematics: 11–16.* K M Hart (Ed). John Murray. 1981 for further discussion of addition items including one of this type (pages 25–27).

21(R)*

The signpost at the junction shows that it is 18 km to Newtown and 23 km to Upton.

How far is it from Newtown to Upton along this road?

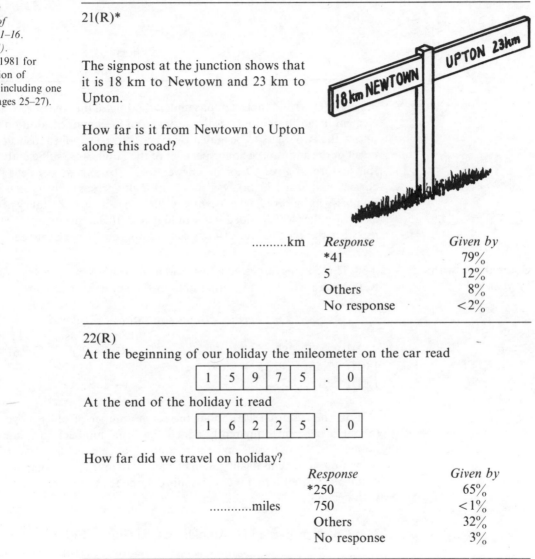

..........km

Response	Given by
*41	79%
5	12%
Others	8%
No response	<2%

22(R)
At the beginning of our holiday the mileometer on the car read

1	5	9	7	5	.	0

At the end of the holiday it read

1	6	2	2	5	.	0

How far did we travel on holiday?

..........miles

Response	Given by
*250	65%
750	<1%
Others	32%
No response	3%

3.28 21 and 22(R) are items illustrating pupils' performance in addition and subtraction in two "everyday" contexts. In response to 21(R), 12 per cent of the pupils used the wrong operation while 79 per cent gave the correct answer. The context of 22(R) proved more difficult and the correct response was given by 65 per cent. It was thought that some pupils might attempt to subtract 16225.0 from 15975.0 because it was placed below the latter but, in fact, only one or two did this.

23(H)

	Response	Given by
(a) 5 + ... = 0	*−5	69%
	0	9%
	Others	5%
	No response	17%
(b) 7 + ... = 7	*0	81%
	−7	5%
	Others	3%
	No response	10%

3.29 23(H) (a) and (b) test pupils understanding of the role of zero as an identity element in addition. But they also differ from the standard addition items in that one of the two digits to be added together is to be supplied instead of being the result of the addition. About 5 per cent of the pupils were sufficiently confused by this feature to give −7 as the answer to 23 (b), but 81 per cent provided the correct response. 23 (a) was more difficult, presumably because a negative number was involved. 69 per cent gave the correct answer while 9 per cent gave 0 as the number which added to 5 would give 0. It is noteworthy that the omission rates for these items were 10 per cent (23b) and 17 per cent (23a).

Comparison with 11 year olds

3.30 Three items discussed above had also been given to 11 year olds and there were others which were comparable in the surveys of primary and secondary pupils.

Facilities (omission rates in brackets)

	15 year olds	11 year olds
17(H) 9417 − 283	83% (5%)	67% (3%)
18(H) 12.45 + 127.5 + 5.691	69% (4%)	37% (14%)
19(H) 5.07 − 1.3	64% (9%)	37% (10%)

3.31 In the case of 18(H) about the same number of older as younger pupils (about 5 per cent) apparently added the four numbers ignoring the decimal points. The 15 year olds made a greater advance over the 11 year old levels in response to the items dealing with decimals (18 and 19) as compared with whole numbers (17), although there was more scope for improvement in performance with decimals.

3.32 One item given to 11 year olds was the same as 13(H) (see paragraph 3.21), except that the fifth number in the addition, 11.65, was not included. Nevertheless, carrying was required in three columns and it is this feature which probably has as much influence on the difficulty of the calculation as the length of the sum involved. 83 per cent of the 11 year olds were successful compared to 91 per cent of the older pupils.

Ratio and proportion

3.33 This section discusses a selection of items which involve ratio and proportion in a variety of contexts, such as scale and cogs.

24(J)   If a distance of 100 km is shown on a map by a line
segment 4 cm long then 1 cm represents

		Response selected by
A.	20 km	10%
*B.	25 km	77%
C.	45 km	3%
D.	50 km	4%
		Omitted by
		6%

3.34 In 24(J) the ratio involved is numerically very simple, but is set in a context of readings from a map. The technical term 'scale' is not used here, but an awareness that the ratio of different lengths on the map is the same as the ratio of corresponding distances is required. As can be seen, nearly 80 per cent of the pupils selected the correct alternative. There seems little reason why A was the most popular incorrect answer, except that some pupils perhaps thought that there were 20 fours in 100.

25(K)   Water pours into a pool at a constant rate of 15
gallons every 3 minutes. What is the rate in gallons
per hour?

		Response selected by
A.	75	4%
B.	150	7%
C.	180	10%
*D.	300	76%
		Omitted by
		3%

3.35 Item 25(K) is a more complicated problem involving higher numbers, knowledge of time and a two stage calculation. However, the ratio still reduces to a unitary one which may explain why the proportion correct is almost as high as in 24(J). Here the most common wrong answer was 180 which is 60×3 and is thus probably obtained by pupils who are aware of the need to apply the connection between minutes and hours but choose the wrong numbers to multiply. (180 is also 15×12 but there seems no reason why a pupil should adopt this strategy.)

26(J)   A basic recipe for pastry is
     120 g flour
     30 g margarine
     30 g lard
     pinch of salt
     water
and this will form the bases of 12 jam tarts.
I want to make 30 of these jam tarts.

Fill in the quantities of flour and margarine I must use.

(a) [   ] flour

(b) [   ] margarine

(a) Response	Given by	(b) Response	Given by
*300 g	53%	*75 g	48%
*300	5%	*75	6%
Others	36%	Others	39%
	Omitted by		Omitted by
	6%		7%

27(J)

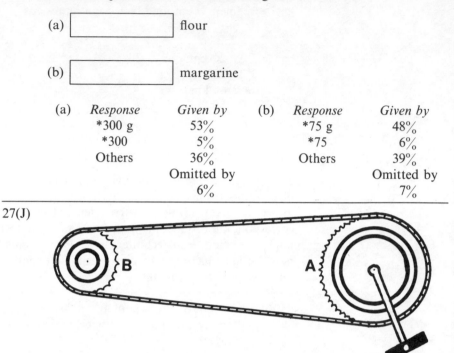

In this picture of the bicycle chain the pedal wheel A has 50 teeth round its edge and the hub wheel B has 20 teeth.

(a) How many times will the hub wheel turn if the pedal wheel goes around twice?

(b) How many times must the pedal wheel go round to make the hub wheel go around 20 times?

(a) Response	Given by	(b) Response	Given by
*5	56%	* 8	41%
4	8%	4	7%
2.5, 2½	8%	50	7%
Other	25%	40	5%
	Omitted by	10	7%
	3%	Other	28%
			Omitted by
			5%

3.36 Items 26 and 27(J) involve a non-unitary, but identical ratio (5:2) in quite different contexts and have similar facilities which are some 20 per cent less than the first two items. 26(J) appears to involve more difficult numbers than 27(J), but it is also easier to decide which way round to use the ratio (more cakes means more flour) and it is possible that these two factors balance each other out. A question similar to 26(J) was used in the 1979 primary survey, but the easier ratio used, 3:1, was enough to enable around 65 per cent of the 11 year olds to get it right.

3.37 In item 27(J), several pupils appear to have been working with a factor of 2, rather than $2\frac{1}{2}$. In part (a), 8 per cent gave the answer 4, while in (b) a similar proportion halved 20 to get 10. In addition, another 5 per cent obtained the answer 40, which still uses a factor of 2, only in the wrong direction. The reason for using 2 could be that some pupils have most experience of working ratio problems which only involve a ratio of 2; on the other hand some may have decided by eye that one wheel looked twice the size of the other. In (b), a further 7 per cent used the ratio the wrong way round to obtain an answer of 50, while in (a) the response 2.5 or $2\frac{1}{2}$ was probably obtained by dividing 50 by 20.

28(J) If a jug holds 300 ml when $\frac{5}{6}$ full how many millilitres does it hold when $\frac{3}{4}$ full?

		Response selected by
A.	240	21%
*B.	270	45%
C.	320	15%
D.	400	10%
		Omitted by 9%

29(J) At the rate of 528 miles in $1\frac{1}{3}$ hours how many miles will a plane fly in $5\frac{1}{2}$ hours?

		Response selected by
A.	1280	5%
*B.	2178	37%
C.	2904	35%
D.	3872	15%
		Omitted by 8%

3.38 Items 28 and 29(J) again involve similar operations in a different context. Apart from the different context, 29(J) also involves mixed numbers which make the ratio rather more difficult to handle and this probably contributes to the slight fall in facility from 28 to 29(J). In 28(J), there seems no obvious reason in terms of ratios why pupils should choose either A or C, (240 is in fact $\frac{4}{5} \times 300$, and 320 is $\frac{16}{15} \times 300$) so there may be other ways in which pupils tackle this problem which cannot be observed with its multiple-choice format. D, on the other hand, which is $300 \times \frac{4}{3}$, and can be obtained by ignoring the first fraction and incorrectly using the second, was chosen least often. In 29(J), which was answered correctly by 37 per cent, nearly as many, 35 per cent, chose alternative C ($528 \times 5\frac{1}{2}$) which can be obtained by ignoring the first time and assuming that the plane is flying at 528 miles per hour. Alternative D, which can be obtained by multiplying 528 by both $1\frac{1}{3}$ and $5\frac{1}{2}$, rather than dividing by $1\frac{1}{3}$ and multiplying by

$5\frac{1}{2}$, was selected by 15 per cent of the pupils. It is interesting to note that the proportion of pupils who omitted items 24(J) to 29(J) was always less than 10 per cent whether or not the item was multiple-choice, even though the facilities showed that pupils found them of varying difficulty. This suggests that the vast majority of pupils found all of these questions familiar enough to attempt, but that there were some elements in the later ones which some pupils were unable to cope with.

30(J)

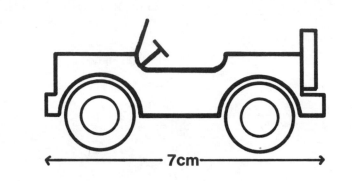

7cm

This model jeep is 7 cm long.
A real jeep is 3.85 metres long.

What is the scale of the model?

Response	Given by
*1:55	
*1 cm:.55 m	} 18%
*55:1	3%
*$\frac{1}{55}$	5%
*7:385	2%
55 with decimal point anywhere	10%
Other	35%
	Omitted by
	27%

3.39 In contrast to the previous items, item 30 not only has a lower facility, 28 per cent, but is also omitted by 27 per cent. The larger proportion of pupils not answering this question is probably due to the term 'scale' which has been introduced here. Although the idea in 30(J) is similar to that in 24(J), the term scale was not used in 24(J), and the numbers are also more difficult in 30(J). These facts, together with the conversion of metres into centimetres, presumably account for many of the incorrect answers. The 10 per cent of the pupils who gave an answer involving the figures 55 realised that one length had to be divided into the other but did not express it as a ratio (and possibly also failed to make the correct units conversion).

31(J)   If you can buy 8.55 French francs for £1, how much is one franc worth in English money to the nearest 1p?

Response	Given by
*12	20%
11	8%
855 with decimal	
point anywhere	4%
Other	43%
	Omitted by
	25%

3.40 A similar proportion of pupils, 25 per cent, omitted 31(J). The division involved is rather awkward, and this is reflected in the lower facility of 20 per cent. The incorrect answer 11 can be obtained in at least two ways: one is after correctly dividing 100 by 8.55 (11.7 to one decimal place) and then making a rounding error to get 11, the other is by rounding 8.55 to 9 and then dividing 100 by 9.

Symbolic representation: conventions

3.41 Different values of mathematical entities such as numbers and measures, and the relationships between them can be represented symbolically. The values are usually represented by letters and the relations and operations by signs (for example $+$, $\times$); the juxtaposition of symbols (for example, xy); brackets; and other typographical devices. This section is concerned with pupils' knowledge of some of these various conventions and the extent to which they are able to distinguish between them. The types of item which test this knowledge include those which involve symbolic representation, and those requiring algebraic expressions to be simplified or evaluated.

Representing relationships

3.42 The results of item 32a(M) show that about 70 per cent of the pupils recognised that if a given symbol represents a value (the age of a person) then the same symbol represents an equal value (the same age of a different person). Items 32(b), 33(a), (b), (c) and 34(M) require a basic relationship ($+$, $\times$, or $-$) to be represented between two symbols. Each of these items obtained a facility of around 45 per cent.

3.43 The errors made in response to these items, and also to 35(M), suggest that some pupils think that an addition is represented by juxtaposing symbols, and a multiplication by using index notation.

3.44 The errors in representation vary with the item. Thus, around 5 per cent juxtaposed symbols instead of using an addition sign in response to 32(b) and 33(a) and (b). The proportion doing this rose to over a third in the case of 34(M) where two letters and no numbers were involved whereas both 32(M) and 33(M) were concerned with one number and one letter.

3.45 In response to item 33(a), those pupils who chose to represent the addition by juxtaposition appear not to have used the number 1 for this purpose and, instead, gave the answer 2n.

32(M)

Peter's age, in years, is represented by x.
If I am exactly the same age as Peter, how can I represent my own age?

(a) Response	Given by
* x years	70%
Others	20%
Omitted by 10%

Alan is exactly two years older than Peter.
How can we represent Alan's age?

(b) Response	Given by
* $x + 2, 2 + x$ years	47%
$2x$	6%
Others	36%
Omitted 11%

33(M)

n represents a whole number.

How do we represent the number which is one bigger than n?

(a) Response	Given by
* $n + 1, 1 + n$	43%
$2n$	4%
Others	36%
Omitted by 17%

How do we represent the number which is three less than n?

(b) Response	Given by
* $n - 3$	43%
$3 - n$	<1%
$-3n$	4%
Others	34%
Omitted by 18%

How do we represent the number which is twice n?

(c) Response	Given by
* $2n, 2 \times n$	42%
n^2	21%
Others	18%
Omitted by 18%

34(M)

I have x pence and you have y pence

How many pence do we have altogether?

Response	Given by
* $x+y, y+x$	46%
xy	34%
Others	12%
Omitted by 8%

3.46 Item 35 involved the representation of two operations and so provided opportunities to make errors in representing multiplication and addition.

†These errors were not coded in 1978 and 1979. The figures given here are from the administration of the item in the 1980 survey. In that survey the item's facility was 58 per cent and the omission rate 8 per cent.

35(M)

A bar of cocolate costs x pence and a packet of crisps costs y pence.

What is the cost of 3 bars of chocolate and one packet of crisps?

	Response	Given by
*	$3x + y$	58%
†	$3xy$	10%
†	expressions with powers e.g.	
	$x^3 + y$, x^3y	9%
†	Any number	7%
†	Others	8%
	Omitted by	9%

3.47 In fact, fewer pupils juxtaposed the symbols than did so in 34(M) and fewer used index notation than did so in 33c(M). The item obtained a higher, not a lower facility than 32, 33 and 34(M). It may be that the two operations involved in 35(M) alerted more pupils to the distinction between the options available for representing relationships than when only one operation is involved.

3.48 Item 36 involved the representation of only one operation but as that operation was division, a different pattern of results was obtained in comparison with the items discussed above. Firstly, as compared with the other one-operation items, a lower proportion of pupils (one-third) gave an acceptable response. An additional 7 per cent, however, knew that a division sign or a fraction line was required but placed the symbols in the wrong order. Some may have done this because they treat division as commutative.

36(M)

The cost of x packets of sweets is 90 pence.

Write down the cost of a single packet.

	Response	Given by
*	$\dfrac{90}{x}$	24%
*	$90 \div x$	8%
*	$x \overline{)90}$	1%
	$\dfrac{x}{90}$ or $x \div 90$	7%
	10	15%
	Others	29%
	Omitted by	16%

3.49 In addition, a substantial proportion (15 per cent) gave the numerical response 10 (other numerical responses such as 30 and 90 were given, but only rarely). Presumably this was regarded as a plausible value for a packet of sweets given by those who could not cope with the algebra. Numerical responses were also occasionally given to the other items discussed. In 32(a), for example, there were a few instances of a value being given for Peter's age and the corresponding value of Alan's age then provided.

3.50 The omission rates for all three of the 33(M) items were nearly twice as high as those for 32, 34 and 35(M). This may reflect the differences in context, the latter group having an "everyday" setting despite the abstract nature of the task. Again, 36(M), the division item, does not fit this pattern; it has an "everyday" setting but its omission rate is about the same as for 33(M) which is an abstract task. Perhaps this is because of the particular difficulty pupils have with the operation of division.

Substituting numbers for letters

3.51 Items requiring pupils to substitute numbers in algebraic expressions provide further evidence of representation errors.

3.52 The only item involving juxtaposition of symbols was given in the practical topic on calculators (see Chapter 2). Pupils were asked to estimate the value of v given that $v = u + gt$, and given values for u, g and t. One-third of them added the three values together, presumably because they thought that the juxtaposition of g and t meant addition. The incidence of the error in this item matches that of 34(M), another item involving letters only. However, it is noteworthy that in the practical item, when pupils were asked to use the calculator to work out the value of $u + gt$, about 8 per cent recognised their error and carried out the correct operations.

3.53 An item, 37(U), in the traditional algebra sub-category involved index notation. 16 per cent of the pupils interpreted the index as a multiplying factor and this compares with the 21 per cent who did so in response to 33c(M). The facility and omission rate for this item were about the same as for 32a(M) and also for the parts of 33(M), each of which involved one number and one letter.

37(U)

			Response		Given by
$y = d^3$					
Find y if $d = 3$		$y =$	27	*	44%
			9		16%
			Other		26%
					Omitted by
					15%

3.54 The items in 38 were given to 11 year old pupils. Although few of the 11 year olds would have had extensive experience of algebraic notation, 90 per cent of the pupils attempted the items and about half of these interpreted the indices as multiplying factors. This error was four times more frequent than in the cases where indices were added to the value of the variable. Apparently there is a strong initial tendency to treat indices as multiplying factors.

---

38 (Primary)

If E stands for 3, then

(a) E^2 stands for ....

(b) E^3 stands for ....

Responses:

		Given by			*Given by*
(a) *	9	16%	(b) *	27	13%
	6	48%		9	46%
	5	11%		6	13%
	Others	15%		Others	18%
		Omitted by			Omitted by
		9%			10%

3.55 Finally it is notable that the success rate for 39(H), which involves numbers only, was greater than that for other items in this section and that the incidence of wrong interpretation declined. However it is not clear whether this improvement was due to numbers only being used or whether pupils were more familiar with the index 2.

39(H)

Write the value of the expression in the space provided to make the statement true.

$$10^2 = ...$$

	Response	*Given by*
*	100	66%
*	10×10	7%
	20	10%
	Others	6%
	Omitted by	
	11%	

Simplifying algebraic expressions

3.56 Items requiring expressions to be simplified generally obtained higher facilities than those concerned with representation and substitution. The incidence of representation errors varied with certain features of the items. 40(i) (M) had the highest success rate (75 per cent) of this group: only one letter was involved and two numerical coefficients. The facility dropped to 65 per cent when one of the two numerical coefficients was 1 in 40(ii). This difficulty with a coefficient of unity, already noted in relation to item 33, raised the incidence of the representation error in 40(ii). In 40(iii) and (iv) no numerical coefficients were given; the facilities and incidences of representation errors were similar to those of 40(i).

---

†The items in 40(M) were paired and presented together in different tests, they have been collected together here for interpretative purposes. The paired items were: (i) and (v); (ii) and (iii); (iv) and (vi).

40(M)†

Item	Response	Given by	Item	Response	Given by
(i) $2a+3a$	*5a	75%	(ii) $a+3a$	*4a	65%
	5a²	6%		3a²	12%
				a⁴	2%
	Others	13%		Others	14%
	Omitted	7%		Omitted	7%
(iii) $a+a+a$	*3a, 3 × a	64%	(iv) $a×a×a$	*a³	61%
	a³	17%		3 × a, 3a	15%
	Others	12%		Others	17%
	Omitted	7%		Omitted	7%
(v) $a+a+b$	*2a+b	55%	(vi) $a×a×b$	*a²b	58%
	a²+b	10%		a²+b	2%
	2ab	5%		2ab	14%
	Others	20%		Others	17%
	Omitted	10%		Omitted	9%

3.57 The introduction of a second variable in 40(v) and (vi) lowered the facility to under 60 per cent and induced two types of representation error, the incidences of which are reversed in the two items.

3.58 It would appear from the 40(M) group of items that there was a tendency to represent continuous addition with index notation instead of juxtaposition, and continuous multiplication with juxtaposition. These items were concerned with the basic relationships between addition and multiplication and between multiplication and index notation. Continuous addition was correctly represented as juxtaposition ($a+a=2a$) and continuous multiplication with index notation ($a×a=a^2$). This suggests that the source of pupils' errors in the representation and substitution type of item lies in their understanding of these basic relationships.

Angles

3.59 The idea of an angle, the comparison, estimation and measurement of the sizes of angles, and the relationships between angles of geometric figures are important features of spatial concepts.

41(P)   Which of these angles is the largest?   ....

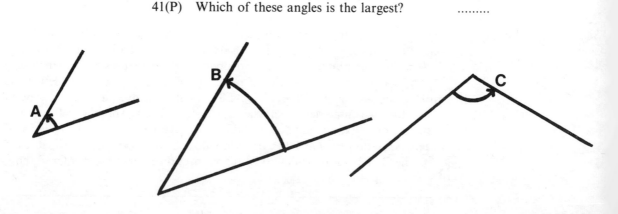

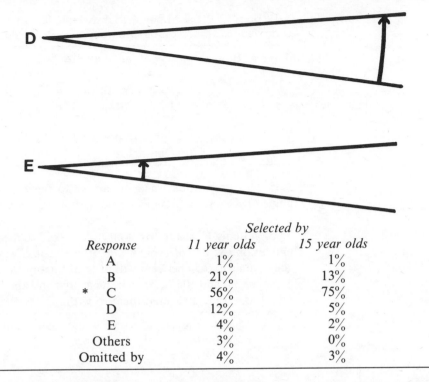

		Selected by
Response	*11 year olds*	*15 year olds*
A	1%	1%
B	21%	13%
* C	56%	75%
D	12%	5%
E	4%	2%
Others	3%	0%
Omitted by	4%	3%

3.60 In 41(P) pupils' understanding of angle size was tested by asking them to select the largest of five angles which vary in their orientation, the lengths of the lines forming them, and the sizes of the arcs which label the relevant angle in each figure. 75 per cent picked out the largest angle correctly, and 13 per cent of the remaining pupils chose angle B, which had the largest labelling arc. A further 5 per cent selected angle D which has the longest lines: it also has a larger arc than angle E, which has bounding lines of about the same length as those of angle D, and which was chosen by 2 per cent.

3.61 It would appear that a fifth of the pupils (those who selected angle B or angle D as the largest) based their judgement of size on prominent features of the figures which are irrelevant to the sizes of the angles. This finding may be related to a finding which emerged from the practical topic, namely that "around 30 per cent defined an angle as the distance, area or space between two lines........".

3.62 Items given to 11 year olds suggest that about three quarters of them can also select a specific angle from given alternatives, at least if the arcs labelling the angles are of equal sizes (see the first primary survey report (page 25)). However, the administration of item 41(P) to the younger pupils demonstrated that when their choice was made from figures which varied on features irrelevant to angle size, their success rate was lowered by nearly 20 per cent. The improvement between 11 and 15 was due to fewer pupils selecting B and D, the angles with the largest arc and longest lines respectively.

3.63 The omission rates for these types of item at both age levels were around 5 per cent.

3.64 Item 42(P) asked pupils to draw an angle of 55° using a protractor. It was completed with acceptable accuracy by 73 per cent.

42(P)   Draw accurately an angle of size 55°.

*Accurate drawing (±1°) made by	73%
Less accurate (±5°)	4%
Inaccurate	17%
Other responses	1%
Omitted by	5%

3.65 This proportion was comparable to the numbers drawing an acceptable angle of 70° in the practical topic without using a protractor (see Chapter 2).

3.66 In items 43(a) and (b) pupils were asked to measure an acute angle of $38\frac{1}{2}°$ and an obtuse one of 116°. About 70 per cent gave a measure within $1\frac{1}{2}°$ of the acute angle and 56 per cent within 1° of the obtuse angle. In the practical topic angles of 33° and 106° were to be measured and about 70 per cent of those pupils taking the topic measured them to within 1° of their actual values.

43(P)   Measure the sizes of each of these angles to the nearest degree. Write your measurements in the spaces provided below each angle.

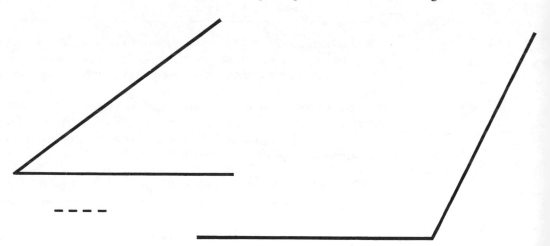

	Response	Given by		Response	Given by
(a)	*38°	17%	(b)	*116°	37%
	*$38\frac{1}{2}°$	1%		*115° or 117°	19%
	*39°	35%		60°–80°	19%
	37° or 40°	18%		Others	20%
	150°–180°	6%		Omitted by	
	Others	19%		5%	
	Omitted by				
	4%				

3.67 The discrepancy between the proportions accurately measuring the obtuse angles in the two modes is accounted for, but not explained, by the numbers of pupils who gave measures of less than 90°. In the written item 43(b), 19 per cent did so but only 5 per cent did so in the practical. This difference may have been due to the fact that the angle in the written test item was not labelled, but the angles also differed in orientation in the two modes. There are also other presentational and contextual differences between the items in the two modes which may have influenced the results.

3.68 The results for items 42 and 43(P) suggest that rather more than 70 per cent of the secondary pupils have a working understanding of the size of acute angles and that the proportion who can deal with obtuse angles is not far below this figure. Details of the performance of pupils in relation to estimating the size of angles can be found in Chapter 2.

Angles between straight lines

44(P)

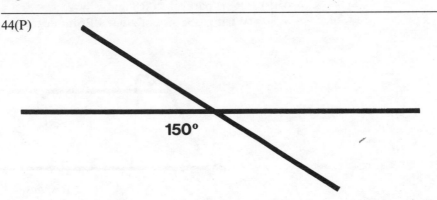

Calculate the sizes of all the other angles where these lines cross and write them in the diagram.

	Given by
*All three correct	61%
150° angle only correct	10%
One 30° angle only correct	1%
150° and one 30° only	1%
Two 30° only	<1%
Other responses	8%
	Omitted by
	19%

3.69 Item 44 is concerned with relations between angles formed by two intersecting lines. 61 per cent of pupils gave the correct values of all three of the unmarked angles, and a further 10 per cent gave only the 150° angle correctly. In the majority of these cases the 150° angle was given alone, but in some cases an incorrect value was also provided for the 30° angles, which suggests that like those who omitted the item, these pupils did not know the relationship between adjacent angles on a straight line. About 3 per cent provided one or two correct values and it is possible that some of these, and some of the pupils who only gave 150°, did not recognise that the values of three angles were required.

3.70 In the primary survey 36 per cent of the pupils gave the correct value of an angle adjacent to one of 150° on a straight line.

3.71 Item 45 involved the concepts of angles on a straight line, corresponding angles, and the representation of angle relationships with algebraic notation. Not surprisingly it was a difficult item, and 17 per cent of pupils gave a value from 63° to 68°. These pupils may well have attempted to measure the angle, for a protractor was supplied to pupils taking the tests which included this item, although it was intended for use in items other than this one. (The actual size of the angle was about 64°.) A further 9 per cent of pupils gave the response 'x'. This, perhaps, indicated that they realised that the angle PRS was equal in size to the one marked 'x' in the diagram but either did not spot its relationship to the one marked '$y°$', or could not cope with the algebra involved.

45(P)　PQ is parallel to RS and y = 2x.
　　　　What is the size of angle PRS in degrees?

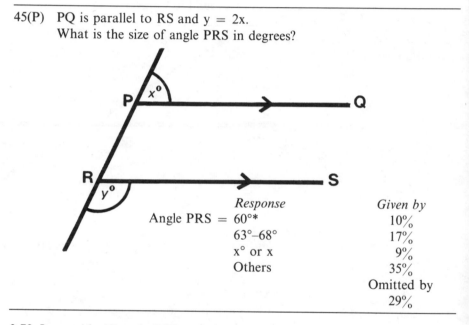

	Response	Given by
Angle PRS =	60°*	10%
	63°–68°	17%
	x° or x	9%
	Others	35%
		Omitted by
		29%

Angles in triangles

3.72 Items 46, 47 and 48(P) tested pupils' knowledge of the angle sum of triangles and their ability to use this knowledge to work out angle sizes in relation to the type of triangle involved.

3.73 Three quarters of the pupils gave the correct value of the third angle of a scalene triangle, given the other two angles (Item 46). The success rate dropped to 53 per cent when pupils were asked for the size of each angle in an equilateral triangle (Item 47). The difference of over 20 per cent in the facilities of these two items could be due to the fact that this proportion of pupils did not know what an equilateral triangle was or did not realise that the three angles must be equal. The omission rate for item 47 (18 per cent) was nearly twice as high as for 46(P) which indicates that some pupils were put off by the form of the question rather than their lack of knowledge of the angle sum of a triangle.

3.74 In the first primary survey 44 per cent of the pupils could correctly supply the value of the third angle of a triangle given the other two.

46(P)

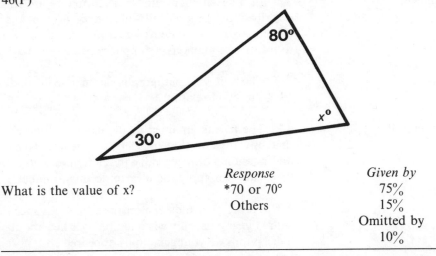

What is the value of x?

Response	Given by
*70 or 70°	75%
Others	15%
	Omitted by
	10%

47(P)

What is the size of each angle in an equilateral triangle?

Response	Given by
*60° or 60	53%
Others	29%
	Omitted by
	18%

48(P)

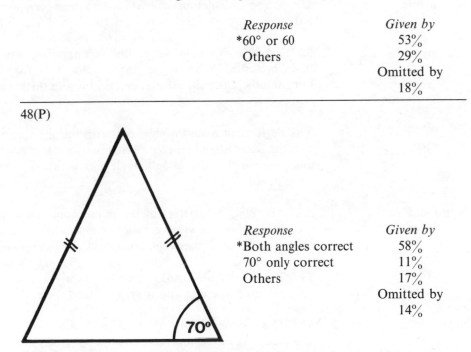

Response	Given by
*Both angles correct	58%
70° only correct	11%
Others	17%
	Omitted by
	14%

Calculate the other two interior angles of this isosceles triangle and write them in the diagram.

3.75 Item 48 concerned the angles of an isosceles triangle. In contrast to the purely verbal presentation of item 47 a diagram was provided and the two equal sides of the triangle indicated. 58 per cent gave the correct values of the two angles which were asked for and a further 11 per cent supplied only one of them – the other base angle.

Summary

3.76 In this chapter pupils' performance in selected topic areas has been described in some detail. The aims of the analyses were to identify the characteristics of test items which are associated with a decline in success rate and to record the main errors and strategies which are apparent in the results.

3.77 The following paragraphs summarise the findings which emerged from the 1979 survey in relation to these aims.

Numeration

3.78 The results obtained by pupils on the numeration items provide evidence that upwards of threequarters of the pupils have a good knowledge and understanding of place value in relation to whole numbers, while about half of them can also apply the idea to decimal numbers.

3.79 The 15 year olds demonstrate their advance in understanding, compared with 11 year olds, only when indirectly asked about place value. Almost as many older pupils as younger pupils appeared to ignore decimal points if asked to compare numbers less than one with different numbers of decimal places.

Adding and subtracting

3.80 About 90 per cent of the pupils gave correct answers to addition and subtraction calculations in which the numbers were presented vertically, although a subtraction involving decimals had a facility of 82 per cent.

3.81 Facilities of around 80 per cent were obtained in response to whole number items presented in words or horizontally. When decimals were involved in horizontally presented calculations there was a further drop in facility to about 65 per cent.

3.82 Performance was lower when the operations were not given in the question, as in the signpost and mileometer items. The role of zero as an identity, tested in questions which involved only single digit numbers, also proved troublesome to some pupils.

Ratio and proportion

3.83 About three-quarters of the pupils could deal with unitary ratios. The proportion of pupils who were successful was below 60 per cent for non-unitary ratios and below 50 per cent when fractions were involved.

3.84 The success rates also depended on a variety of factors such as the size of the numbers used, the operations involved and the context.

Symbolic representation: conventions

3.85 This section was mainly concerned with errors made in representing and interpreting relationships between symbols. Items involving representation, and those concerned with substituting in and simplifying algebraic expressions were discussed.

3.86 The incidence of representation errors apparently increases in relation to the number of different symbols used. The incidence of juxtaposition interpreted as or representing an addition rose to about one-third of the pupils when only abstract symbols were involved in the question. The incidence of indices being interpreted as multiplying factors was higher than the former error, relative to which symbols were used. A strong early tendency to make this latter error is revealed by the responses of 11 year old pupils to substitution items.

3.87 Particular difficulties were also noted with representing division and also with expressions containing numerical coefficients one of which is unity.

Angles

3.88 This section discussed the results of items concerned with comparing and measuring angles and with pupils' knowledge of the relationships among angles between straight lines and within triangles. About 70 – 75 per cent can compare and measure angles, but the evidence of both written and practical items suggests that a significant proportion of pupils are unaware of the defining features of 'angle'. About 60 per cent know the basic facts about angles between straight lines and 75 per cent the angle sum of triangles – in each case about 30 per cent more than among 11 year old pupils. However, if these basic relationships are employed in conjunction with others (for example in equilateral or isosceles triangles) then the facilities fall. It is not clear whether this is because the relevance of the other relationships is not appreciated or whether the basic relationships cannot be applied in more complex contexts.

4 The written tests: sub-category scores and background variables

The Sub-category scores

4.1 In this chapter, the pattern of performance in each of the sub-categories in the 1979 written tests is described in relation to the various groupings of the background variables. In order to do this, a sub-category score had to be obtained for each pupil so that mean scores could be calculated for all the various sub-divisions of the sample.

4.2 As described in Chapter 3, each test contained parts from three sub-categories and each sub-category was usually divided into five such parts. In order to obtain an overall score for each sub-category, each pupil's performance on the respective sub-category was converted into a score on a common scale[1] and these scores were then averaged across all the children who took each sub-category. Mean scores for the different groupings of the background variables were obtained by averaging across the pupils within the appropriate grouping.

4.3 When the tests were constructed, the different sub-category parts were made as nearly equal in overall difficulty as was possible but, no matter how carefully this is done, there will always be some variation in their difficulties, however slight. The technique of scaling enables allowance to be made for possible variation in the difficulties of the different sub-category parts.

4.4 It should be noted that this scaling is only done within each sub-category so that there is, in effect, a different scale for each sub-category. As a result, no educational significance should be attached to differences between the overall mean sub-category scores presented in this report.

4.5 Figure 4.1 shows the relationship between the scaled scores reported in this chapter and the more familiar way of expressing test scores as a percentage of correct responses. The figure provides an approximate conversion of the scaled scores into their equivalents in terms of the percentage of items in the sub-category which would be answered correctly if all the items were used as a single test. Thus a mean scaled score of 50 implies that 50 per cent of the items would be answered correctly by the average pupil. A mean scaled score of 45 implies that just over 30 per cent of the items would be answered correctly by such a pupil, and so on. In addition, it can be seen from Figure 4.1 that the majority of scaled scores are likely to lie in the range from 35 to 65 scaled units since this band covers the range of 5–95 per cent of items answered correctly.

The background variables

4.6 In this section, performance is described in relation to five characteristics of the schools in the sample. These are:

1. Percentage of pupils taking free school meals
2. Pupil/teacher ratio

[1] The scaling procedure used is derived from the Rasch model. For a more detailed account of its use in analysing the data from the mathematics surveys see Appendix 3 in *Mathematical Development. Primary survey report No. 2.* HMSO, 1981.

Figure 4.1   *Showing the relationship between the scaled scores and the percentage of items which would be answered correctly if all the items in the sub-category were used as a single test.*

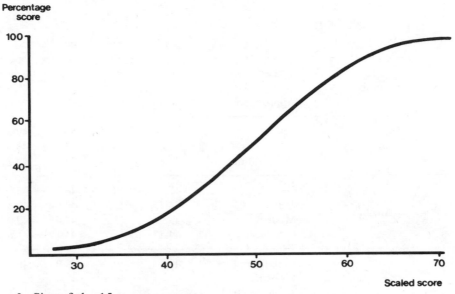

3. Size of the 15+ age group
4. Location in a metropolitan or non-metropolitan authority
5. Region of the country

Separate data for boys and girls are also reported.

4.7 Table 4.1 shows the scaled scores obtained by the pupils in each grouping of the background variables for each sub-category, as well as the scores of the whole sample. In addition, the differences between the mean scaled scores obtained by the pupils in each grouping of the background variables and the mean scaled score obtained for all the pupils who took the sub-category in 1979 are shown in graphical form in Figures 4.2 to 4.6. In each case an indication is given of the 95 per cent confidence limits, that is, the range within which these differences are most likely to lie for the total population. For example, in Figure 4.5, the mean difference score in the number concepts sub-category for the sample schools in the South of England is shown as $+0.6$ (from Table 4.1: $55.4 - 54.8 = 0.6$) while the range within which the mean score for the South is likely to lie is -0.1 to $+1.4$.

4.8 It is useful as a rule of thumb to note those occasions where there is only a small overlap, or none at all, between two sets of confidence limits. In these cases the discrepancy between the two mean scores concerned is so large that it is unlikely to have arisen solely from sampling fluctuations and is thus likely to be significant in the statistical sense (see Appendix 2).

Free school
meals

4.9 This analysis relates to schools in the maintained sector. To gain an indication of the affluence of a school's catchment area, the number of pupils taking free school meals on a particular day was expressed as a percentage of the total number of pupils taking school meals on the same day.

Table 4.1 *Mean scaled scores for each sub-category and background variable†*

			Free school meals* %			Pupil/teacher** ratio		
		All	<15	15—29.9	≥30	<15	15—17.4	≥17.5
Number	Concepts	54.8	56.9	53.9	52.8	53.4	54.7	54.7
	Skills	51.8	53.4	51.5	49.6	51.0	51.5	51.6
	Applications	48.8	50.5	48.4	46.4	48.1	48.6	48.4
Measures	Unit	51.9	53.6	51.7	49.7	51.6	51.7	51.7
	Rate and ratio	44.6	46.0	43.8	43.5	43.3	44.7	44.3
	Mensuration	44.6	46.3	44.1	42.7	43.5	44.4	44.7
Algebra	General	47.7	50.2	46.7	45.0	46.8	47.7	46.8
	Traditional	44.7	46.7	44.0	42.3	44.2	44.6	44.0
	Modern	43.9	45.5	43.4	42.0	42.8	44.0	43.1
	Graphical	44.5	46.7	44.1	41.6	43.5	44.4	43.9
Geometry	Descriptive	48.6	50.7	48.0	46.4	47.0	48.5	48.5
	Modern	42.1	44.5	41.4	39.4	41.6	42.0	41.6
	Trigonometry	41.7	43.5	40.7	40.1	41.1	41.9	40.8
Probability and Statistics	Probability	46.0	47.7	45.5	44.0	45.8	45.9	45.7
	Statistics	47.3	49.0	47.0	45.3	47.6	47.2	46.9

†The mean scores shown here have been scaled and no direct comparisons can therefore be made with Table 4.1 in Secondary Survey Report No. 1 where mean scores were shown as percentages.

*Maintained schools only.

4.10 The sampled schools were divided into three groups as follows:

Group taking free school meals	*Percentage of pupils in the maintained school sample*
(i) less than 15%	34
(ii) between 15 and 30%	36
(iii) 30% and over	30

4.11 Figure 4.2 indicates that there was a strong association between performance and this variable. Scores in group (i) were higher, and significantly so, than scores in group (ii) in every sub-category and scores in group (ii) were also higher than scores in group (iii) in every sub-category, significantly so in 13 out of the 15.

4.12 When this variable was looked at in relation to the other background variables, it was found that scores in the three groups were always ordered in the same way, but that the size of the differences often varied. For example, in relation to school size it was found that the differences were twice as great in small schools as in large schools; greatest in Northern Ireland and least in Wales, greatest in schools with the most favourable staffing ratio and least in schools with the least favourable staffing ratio.

Size of 15+ age group***				Location		Region					Sex	
1–145	146–205	206–265	266+	Non-Met.	Met.	North	Mid.	South	Wales	N.I.	Boys	Girls
54.3	54.7	54.1	55.1	55.5	53.6	54.4	54.3	55.4	53.9	55.0	55.0	54.6
52.1	51.5	51.2	51.8	52.4	50.7	51.7	51.2	52.4	50.1	52.9	52.0	51.7
49.2	48.3	48.1	48.7	49.2	48.0	48.2	48.2	49.7	47.1	48.8	49.5	48.0
52.4	51.1	52.0	51.8	52.4	51.1	51.6	51.3	52.6	50.7	51.6	53.0	50.8
45.3	43.9	43.9	44.9	45.0	43.8	44.5	44.5	44.8	43.9	44.3	45.6	43.4
45.2	43.8	43.9	45.0	45.2	43.5	44.6	44.6	44.8	43.3	44.3	45.4	43.7
48.6	46.7	46.8	47.5	48.2	46.7	47.4	47.3	48.1	47.5	48.6	48.0	47.4
45.8	44.1	43.6	44.3	45.5	43.3	44.3	43.5	45.7	44.4	45.8	44.9	44.6
44.0	43.4	43.1	44.1	44.5	42.7	43.0	43.9	44.6	42.6	45.0	43.5	44.3
44.8	43.6	43.7	45.1	45.3	43.0	44.0	44.0	45.2	42.9	44.7	45.1	43.8
49.0	48.2	47.9	48.6	49.2	47.7	48.1	48.0	49.5	47.9	47.9	49.1	48.2
42.6	41.1	41.7	42.6	42.7	40.9	41.1	42.0	43.2	40.0	42.1	42.3	41.9
42.8	41.5	40.8	41.3	42.2	40.9	41.6	41.1	42.3	40.9	41.3	42.2	41.2
46.2	46.1	45.9	45.8	46.6	44.9	45.5	45.4	47.0	43.5	45.6	46.1	45.9
47.6	47.0	46.8	47.9	47.7	46.6	47.0	47.1	48.0	44.4	47.1	47.4	47.2

**Maintained schools in England and Wales only.

***Results shown here for size of 15+ age group relate only to maintained schools in England. Results for maintained schools in Wales and Northern Ireland are shown in the section on size of 15+ age group (paragraphs 4.21–4.25).

4.13 When other background variables were analysed, taking into account the affluence of schools' catchment areas, several significant variations were found in the patterns of performance. These are reported here in the relevant sections for those variables.

Pupil/teacher ratio

*Percentages are rounded to the nearest whole number.

4.14 This analysis relates to schools in the maintained sector in England and Wales.

4.15 The sampled schools were divided into three groups according to their pupil/teacher ratio as follows:

	Percentage* of pupils in maintained schools in England and Wales
(i) Schools with a ratio less than 15:1	12
(ii) Schools with a ratio from 15:1 to 17.4:1	58
(iii) Schools with a ratio of 17.5:1 and over	31

Figure 4.2 *Differences from each sub-category's overall mean scaled score for the free school meals variable.*

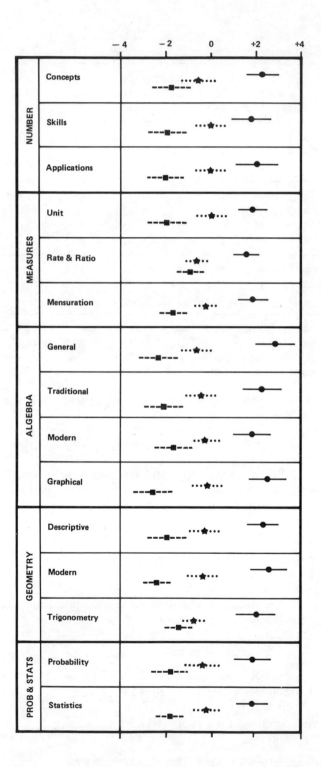

Figure 4.3 *Differences from each sub-category's overall mean scaled score for pupil/teacher ratio.*

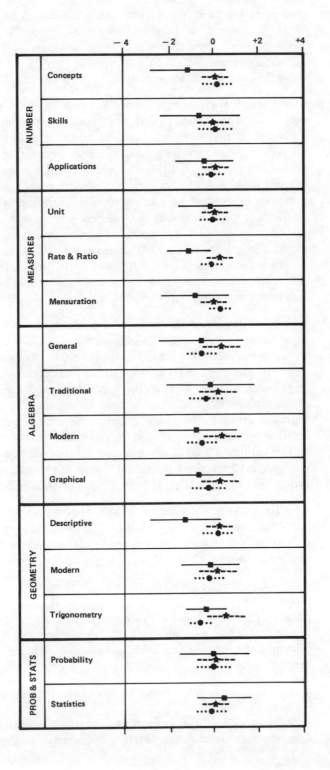
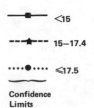

4.16 The results obtained for this variable are illustrated graphically in Figure 4.3. The differences between the three groups were all rather small. Pupils from group (ii) obtained higher scores than group (i) pupils in all but one of the sub-categories, but the difference was significant in only one of them (rate and ratio). Scores in group (ii) were higher than scores in group (iii) in 12 sub-categories, but again only one difference was significant (trigonometry). Although scores in group (iii) were higher than those in group (i) in 10 of the sub-categories, none of these differences was significant.

4.17 Further analyses were carried out to look at this variable in relation to the other background variables. It was found that the pattern of performance was different in the two location groups of schools, metropolitan and non-metropolitan. In non-metropolitan schools, pupils from schools with the most favourable pupil/teacher ratio achieved the highest scores, with pupils in group (ii) and then group (iii) achieving lower scores. In metropolitan schools, this pattern was reversed, with scores increasing through groups (i), (ii) and (iii). In addition, it was found that the difference between scores in metropolitan and non-metropolitan areas noted in the section on school location was much more marked in groups (i) and (ii) than in group (iii). In groups (i) and (ii), the difference was usually over 2 units of scaled score, whereas in group (iii) the difference was around $\frac{1}{2}$ a unit. This variation in the pattern of performance was significant in 9 sub-categories.

4.18 A difference in the pattern of performance was again found when the pupil/teacher ratio variable was looked at in relation to the free school meals variable. For schools in the most affluent areas, performance was highest among pupils in group (i) in 10 sub-categories and tended to decline with increasing pupil/teacher ratios. In contrast, for schools with the least affluent catchment areas, performance tended to increase with an increase in the pupil/teacher ratio, scores in group (ii) being the highest in 8 sub-categories. Also, the difference between overall performance in the most and least affluent schools noted in the section on free school meals occurred within each pupil/teacher ratio band but was greatest for group (i) – around 6 units in most sub-categories – and least for group (iii) – under 2 units. These variations were significant in 13 sub-categories.

4.19 It should be noted that it is the school staffing ratios which are being used here, and the different organisational arrangements adopted by schools mean that these will not necessarily be closely related to the size of mathematics teaching groups.

4.20 It has already been mentioned that the background variables are not all independent and it is clear from the above that interpretation of the data on pupil/teacher ratio is not a straightforward matter. There are probably several inter-related factors underlying the data reported here, and more detailed information needs to be collected in order to investigate these relationships more deeply.

Size of 15-plus age group

4.21 This analysis relates only to schools in the maintained sector.

4.22 The analysis for this variable was carried out separately for England, Wales and Northern Ireland with different boundaries for the four categories because of the different distribution of sizes in the three countries. The size of the age group in schools in this sample in Northern Ireland and Wales tends to be smaller than in England. The results for England appear in Table 4.1 (see pages 66-67) and the results for Wales and Northern Ireland are given in Tables 4.2 and 4.3.

England

Size of 15-plus age group	Percentage of pupils in English sample
(i) 1 – 145	19
(ii) 146 – 205	27
(iii) 206 – 265	26
(iv) 266 +	28

4.23 The differences between the four groups were generally rather small and there was no general trend in performance to vary with size of age group. The overall tendency was for scores in group (i) to be highest, followed by groups (iv), (ii) and (iii) in that order. The differences between (i) and (iv) were never significant, those between groups (iv) and (ii) were significant on 4 sub-categories. None of the differences between groups (ii) and (iii) were significant.

Wales

Size of 15-plus age group	Percentage of pupils in Welsh sample
(i) 1 – 105	19
(ii) 106 – 145	24
(iii) 146 – 225	29
(iv) 226 +	28

Table 4.2 *Mean scaled scores for each sub-category by size of 15-plus age group for Wales.*

		⩽105	106 – 145	146 – 225	⩾226
		1	2	3	4
Number	Concepts	53.7	51.9	55.9	53.0
	Skills	51.4	50.6	51.3	49.0
	Applications	47.9	46.5	48.4	46.1
Measures	Unit	51.9	49.4	53.5	49.1
	Rate and ratio	43.3	42.3	45.2	43.3
	Mensuration	44.4	42.9	44.7	42.3
Algebra	General	45.6	46.4	49.7	46.2
	Traditional	44.6	44.2	47.2	42.6
	Modern	43.2	42.0	43.9	41.5
	Graphical	43.5	42.3	43.9	42.0
Geometry	Descriptive	47.7	47.0	48.9	47.2
	Modern	40.9	39.8	42.0	38.2
	Trigonometry	41.1	39.3	42.1	40.2
Probability and Statistics	Probability	43.4	43.4	44.3	43.0
	Statistics	45.0	43.8	45.0	43.8

4.24 Again, the differences were not large, with the tendency being for pupils from schools in group (iii) to achieve the highest scores, followed consecutively by groups (i), (ii) and (iv). The differences between groups (iii) and (i) were significant on only one sub-category, between (i) and (ii) on two and between (ii) and (iv) on one, whilst the differences between the generally highest and lowest groups, (iii) and (iv), were significant on eight sub-categories.

Northern Ireland

Size of 15-plus age group	Percentage of pupils in N. Ireland sample
(i) 1–75	23
(ii) 76–105	28
(iii) 106–125	17
(iv) 126+	32

4.25 The general picture was that the scores tended to be ordered with group (iv) first followed by groups (ii), (i) and (iii). However, very few of these differences were significant. No graphs have been drawn for size of age group, as the variation in performance was too small for the graphs to be of any interest.

Table 4.3 *Mean scaled scores for each sub-category by size of 15-plus age group for Northern Ireland.*

		≤75	76–105	106–125	>126
		1	2	3	4
Number	Concepts	53.4	55.1	54.3	55.9
	Skills	52.3	52.6	51.2	54.0
	Applications	47.7	48.0	47.5	50.4
Measures	Unit	51.1	51.1	50.2	52.7
	Rate and ratio	43.9	43.4	43.1	45.8
	Mensuration	43.5	44.0	44.1	44.9
Algebra	General	46.8	47.6	47.0	50.6
	Traditional	44.3	45.2	43.9	47.5
	Modern	44.9	44.0	43.7	46.4
	Graphical	43.6	44.1	43.4	46.1
Geometry	Descriptive	47.7	47.4	46.2	48.9
	Modern	41.5	40.9	41.5	43.4
	Trigonometry	40.9	40.4	40.1	42.6
Probability and Statistics	Probability	44.7	45.1	44.7	46.6
	Statistics	46.9	46.4	46.0	48.2

Location

4.26 The results obtained by pupils in metropolitan and non-metropolitan areas are shown in Figure 4.4. It should be noted that education authorities are classified as metropolitan or non-metropolitan according to the nature of their

Figure 4.4 *Differences from each sub-category's overall mean scaled score for school location.*

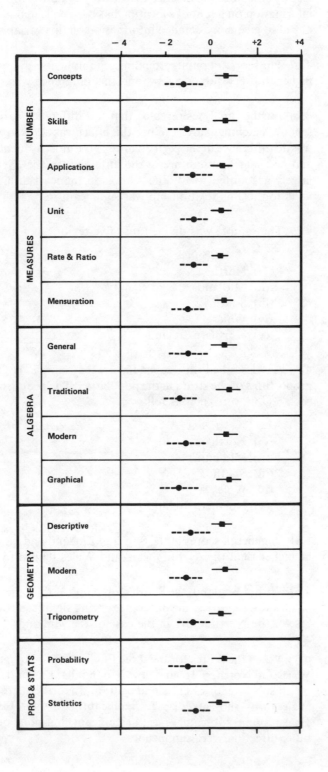

whole area, so that some urban connurbations are not necessarily classified as metropolitan. All the authorities in Wales, for example, are classified as non-metropolitan despite the high density of population in some areas. More detailed information on a school's location has been collected in the 1980 survey and it is hoped to give more detailed information on this variable in a subsequent report.

4.27 The scores of pupils attending schools in non-metropolitan authorities were higher in every sub-category, and this difference was significant in every case.

4.28 Further analyses revealed that this difference varied with the affluence of schools' catchment areas. When this effect was allowed for, it was seen that there was no difference in the performance of the most affluent schools in metropolitan and non-metropolitan areas: the difference in the overall scores tended to be largely accounted for by the schools in the least affluent areas. However, the variation in this relationship was significant in only 4 of the sub-categories.

Region

4.29 The sample was divided into five regions as follows:

Region	Percentage of pupils in the sample
(i) North	21
(ii) Midlands	16
(iii) South	27
(iv) Wales	15
(v) Northern Ireland	21

4.30 As described in Appendix 1, the sample is weighted to reflect the proportions of the strata in the population. The proportions of the population in each region were then as follows:

Region	Percentage of pupils in the population
(i) North	29
(ii) Midlands	21
(iii) South	41
(iv) Wales	5
(v) Northern Ireland	4

4.31 In general, scores in the South of England and Northern Ireland tended to be higher than the overall mean, and Wales tended to have the lowest scores.

4.32 Within England, the South scored higher than the North and the Midlands on all sub-categories, the differences being significant on 9 sub-categories in the case of the North and 7 in the case of the Midlands.

4.33 When the scores for the three English regions together were compared with Wales and Northern Ireland, it was found that England scored higher than Wales on all sub-categories (11 significant) and Northern Ireland scored higher than Wales on 14 sub-categories (7 significant). Northern Ireland scored higher than England on 6 sub-categories (4 significant) but none of the 9 differences in the other direction were significant.

Figure 4.5 *Differences from each sub-category's overall mean scaled score for region.*

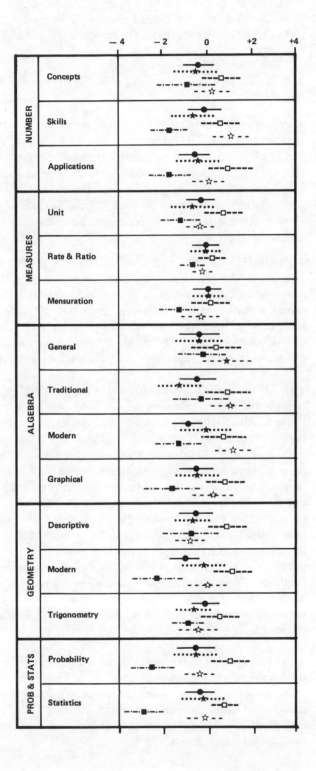

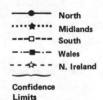

[1] *Mathematical development. Primary survey report No. 2.* HMSO, 1981, price £5.80.

4.34 These variations between countries are rather different from those found in the second primary survey[1] (see Primary survey report No. 2). Here, Wales scored higher than England in many of the primary sub-categories, particularly in number, and the Northern Ireland scores were consistently higher than those in England and Wales, the differences being significant in all but one of the sub-categories.

Sex of pupil

[1] *Achievement in Mathematics,* Pidgeon, D. A. (ed) NFER, 1967.
[2] *Progress in Secondary Schools,* Steedman, J. National Children's Bureau, 1980.

4.35 Scores on each of the sub-categories for boys and girls are shown in Figure 4.6.

4.36 Boys scored higher in 14 sub-categories and the differences were significant in seven of them. The difference in modern algebra, where girls scored higher, was not significant. It was decided to investigate further these sex differences in terms of whether pupils attended single sex or mixed schools. This was prompted by various other studies which had looked at mathematics performance in terms of sex of a school, for example the first IEA Maths Study[1] and the National Child Development Study[2]. The following analyses relate only to schools in the maintained sector.

4.37 The IEA Mathematics Study, carried out in 1965, found that both boys and girls achieved higher mathematics scores in single sex than in mixed schools, and also that the differences between boys and girls were smaller for those attending mixed schools than for those attending single sex schools. The 1979 APU secondary survey agreed with this: boys in single sex schools did better than those in mixed schools in all of the sub-categories (significantly so in seven) and girls did better in single sex schools in eleven sub-categories (with none significant).

[1] *1978 Statistics of Education,* HMSO 1980.

4.38 These results were then looked at in more detail by dividing the schools into two groups—comprehensive schools and other maintained (i.e. grammar and modern schools). In comprehensive schools, there was no difference at all in performance between pupils in single sex and mixed schools for either boys or girls. Just under 15 per cent of the sample pupils who were in comprehensive schools were in single sex comprehensives and, while this is a fairly small proportion, there was no indication that the performances of these pupils were higher. The overall difference between single sex and mixed schools was accounted for entirely by schools in the 'other maintained' group. However, it is likely that at least a large part of this difference is due to the different proportions of grammar and modern schools that are either single sex or mixed: 75 per cent of grammar schools are single sex whereas only 30 per cent of modern schools are single sex[1]. Whether the difference between single sex and mixed schools can be accounted for entirely by the over-representation of grammar school pupils in the single sex schools or whether there is a residual difference due to the sex of a school requires further analysis.

4.39 It is expected that more detailed analyses will be carried out in future when the results of consecutive surveys can be amalgamated. The sample size for a single survey is such that when the 'other maintained' group of schools is further sub-divided into grammar and modern schools, the number of sample pupils in certain of the categories of school type are too small for any meaningful conclusions to be drawn.

Figure 4.6 *Differences from each sub-category's overall mean scaled score for boys and girls.*

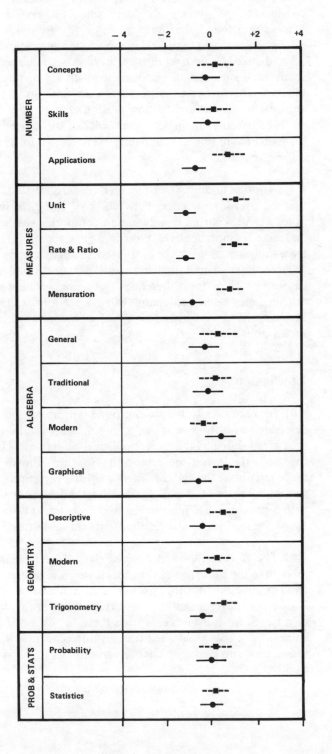

[1]Steedman, op. cit.

4.40 The National Child Development Study[1] was able to look at the position in 1974 in more detail. It found that sex of school was not associated with any difference in performance in comprehensive schools for either boys or girls. In considering the 'other maintained' schools it separated grammar and modern schools and found that girls in single sex grammar schools achieved higher mathematics scores than girls in mixed grammar schools, whereas girls in single sex and mixed modern schools achieved very similar scores. However, for boys it found little variation of performance with sex of school, whether grammar or modern. This last result differs from the findings of the 1979 APU secondary survey where, although within the 'other maintained' group of schools girls performed better in single sex schools, so too did boys. In fact the difference between boys in single sex and mixed schools was on average twice the equivalent difference for girls.

4.41 Another finding which emerged from the 1979 APU secondary survey was that the overall differences between boys' and girls' mathematics performance noted above occurred mainly in non-comprehensive schools. In both single-sex and mixed comprehensives, boys' and girls' scores were virtually the same, apart from in measures where boys still scored slightly higher. In non-comprehensive schools, boys scored higher on all but one (modern algebra) of the sub-categories. Here the differences were greater between boys and girls who attended single-sex non-comprehensive schools (average $3\frac{1}{2}$ scaled units) than between those who attended mixed non-comprehensive schools (average $1\frac{1}{2}$ scaled units).

Conclusion

4.42 In relation to the background variables, performance was strongly associated with the location of a school, and with the affluence of its catchment area as measured by the free school meals variable. Of the regions, Wales tended to obtain the lowest scores and the South of England and Northern Ireland tended to obtain the highest. There was little variation of performance in relation to a school's size of 15-plus age group although there was a tendency for schools with a pupil/teacher ratio in the middle band to obtain slightly higher scores. Boys obtained higher scores than girls on all but one of the sub-categories.

4.43 The picture reported here of overall performance and performance in relation to the background variables is very similar to that reported for 1978. No valid or meaningful comparisons can be made between these two surveys since, even where the results differ, two surveys cannot provide evidence of the presence of a trend. Such evidence, if such there be, cannot be produced until further surveys have been conducted and any differences between 1978 and 1979 can be shown either to be due to chance variation or to be part of a general long-term trend.

5 Attitudes towards mathematics

Introduction

[1] 'Attitudes toward mathematics,' Aiken, L. R. in *Review of educational research*, 40, 1970, 551–596.

[2] 'Women and girls in mathematics,' Fennema, E. in *educational studies in mathematics*, 10, 1979, 389–401.

[3] 'Schooling and sex roles: the case of GCE 'O' level mathematics,' Sharma, S. and Meighan, R. *British Journal of Sociology of Education*, 1, 2, 1980, 193–204.

[4] Fennema, E. op. cit.

5.1 The full extent to which attitudes toward mathematics affect performance is unclear. Those who have investigated the question have consistently reported a positive but moderate relationship between the two, indicating a reciprocal influence. On the other hand, scores on attitude scales have shown little predictive power in relation to performance. Finding mathematics a useful and interesting subject does not necessarily imply high attainment. What, then, is the justification for assessing attitudes? Aside from the more general educational and social aims that involve positive attitudes toward mathematics, there are specific reasons for their assessment. One is the indirect influence that they exert upon performance. For example, it is generally conceded that attitudes affect the persistence of pupils when faced with what may appear to be a difficult subject[1]. They also affect the amount of mathematics that pupils will elect to study[2]. Both persistence and mathematical experience have, in turn, been regarded as predictive of performance. That the number of mathematics-related courses taken by pupils is a strong indicator of achievement in mathematics was confirmed in a recent analysis of one set of O-level mathematics papers. It was found that the greater part of the variance in attainment among candidates could be explained by differences in mathematical-related experiences in other subjects (for example physics and geometric drawing)[3]. It has also been suggested that survey results in the United States which have indicated a relatively lower mathematics performance on the part of girls can be accounted for by sex differences in the amount of mathematics courses taken[4]. In addition to this evidence for the indirect effect of attitudes on performance, there is a pragmatic justification for their investigation in that detailed analysis can be used to isolate areas of concern.

5.2 Early efforts to construct valid measures tended to rely upon the summation of pupils' responses to statements incorporating a range of specific attitudes, such as interest, usefulness, difficulty, anxiety, etc. The result was a single score measuring a general predisposition toward the subject. Although indicative of feelings and beliefs that directed behaviour, the results of such assessment had little practical value to the educator. However, in recent years research into attitudes has become increasingly specific both in terms of the measure itself and the focal behaviour. The tendency to view attitude as a generalised feeling toward a particular object or situation has been replaced by the recognition that attitudes themselves are complex, influenced by factors that are often untapped by conventional unidimensional scales. As a result, attention has turned away from the measurement of generalised predispositions to the investigation of the components of attitude. Not only is such work considered to be more predictive of specific behaviour, but it also allows researchers to investigate those aspects of attitude that may be amenable to change and influence.

5.3 This approach seems particularly appropriate to secondary school pupils. Although perceptions of 'mathematics' may differ among primary school pupils depending upon the interests and concerns of their teachers, at secondary level there is a large divergence among pupils, both in terms of curriculum and 'mathematical content'. For these pupils, the term 'maths' has a multitude of connotations. There is no consensus on what pupils are referring to when we ask them about their feelings towards the subject. Their perception may differ according to their most immediate experience. On the other hand, intuitively it would seem that there exists a common core of activities and types of thought processes that are typical of mathematics as distinct from other subjects. Mathematics is not only a series of topics, but a discipline within the school curriculum. As such, it is likely to evoke a general predisposition toward the subject as a whole as well as positive or negative feeling towards its constituent activities.

5.4 This survey has attempted to investigate both these aspects of attitude towards mathematics. By presenting statements which express opinions concerning the utility, enjoyment and difficulty of mathematics, the survey has attempted to measure a general predisposition towards the subject. Although agreement or disagreement with such statements may correlate only moderately with performance, they do give some indication of pupils' feelings and may highlight aspects of feeling that might otherwise be ignored. By asking pupils to consider specific topics, activities and actual written items, the survey has attempted to define the components of the curriculum that pupils find difficult, useful and interesting. Certainly, this is the more pragmatic aspect of the survey, designed to identify areas of concern for those involved in mathematics education. Finally, through a series of interviews and open-ended questions, the survey has attempted to capture individual insights into the quantitative results obtained from the other measures.

Description of the questionnaire and its administration

5.5 The questionnaire consisted of four sections:

1. A set of questions asking pupils about their favourite school subjects, their feelings towards mathematics and, in particular, those aspects of mathematics which they found difficult and/or useful.

2. A set of 34 statements expressing positive and negative opinions about mathematics. Pupils were asked to indicate the extent of their agreement or disagreement with each statement. Responses were coded and summed to form three scores measuring the degree to which they found mathematics useful, enjoyable and difficult.

3. A list of 17 mathematical topics and activities covering a wide range of the mathematics curriculum. Pupils were asked to rate each in terms of usefulness and interest.

4. 15 items chosen from the written survey. Pupils were asked to attempt each item and then to rate "this type of problem" in terms of its difficulty, interest and usefulness.

5.6 The questionnaire was the synthesis of several earlier versions which had been tried out in the spring of 1979. By that time, previous research concerning attitudes toward mathematics had been reviewed and a provisional questionnaire had been constructed. However, problems of order and content remained to be settled. Before administering the questionnaire to the survey sample it was necessary to examine three distinct aspects of test validity: the internal cohesion of a set of statements which could be used to form scales of attitude towards mathematics; the validity of the topic names which had been chosen to represent the mathematics curriculum; and the effect of order of presentation of the various sections on pupils' response. As a result of these considerations, four versions of the questionnaire were constructed. All were structurally similar to each other, and to the final version, but varied in order of presentation and content.

5.7 These pilot versions were administered to 269 pupils in 12 randomly selected schools. In order to cover a range of ability and, at the same time, to simplify administration, these schools were asked to choose an English language class of average ability. All pupils in these classes were given one of four versions of the pilot questionnaire. In a further attempt to ensure the appropriateness of the questionnaire to the concerns of pupils, a series of group discussions was carried out in 6 of the 12 schools. While maintaining individual anonymity, pupils were given the opportunity to comment upon their attitudes towards mathematics in general, towards specific mathematical topics and towards the questionnaire in particular.

5.8 On the basis of these discussions and the subsequent statistical analysis, the content of the questionnaire was rationalised and its final form agreed upon. Two versions were eventually presented in the survey. These were identical except for the order in which the attitude scales appeared. In one version, the scales were placed immediately following the introductory questions. In the second, they came after the section requiring the completion of the test items. This variation was introduced to ensure that the responses to the general scales were reliable and basically unaffected by any immediate response to what could be considered a testing situation.

5.9 A similar problem occurred in reference to the written tests vis-a-vis the attitude questionnaire. As a precaution against the possible distortion of normal attitudes towards mathematics by the relative ease or difficulty of the written tests, the questionnaire was administered to pupils before they had been informed that they had been selected for the survey sample.

5.10 The results reported in the following chapter are based on the responses of approximately 900 pupils from 170 schools. All of these pupils later took one of the written tests, allowing for the comparison of attitude and performance within the sample.

[1]Details of the development of the scales are contained in Appendix 4.

Attitudes toward mathematics: the scales[1]

5.11 General attitudes toward mathematics were measured by the responses of pupils to 34 statements expressing opinions about mathematics, and in particular concerning the enjoyment offered by mathematical activities, the utility of learning mathematics and its difficulty. Pupils were asked to indicate the extent of their agreement with each statement by ticking one of the 5 categories ranging from "strongly agree" to "strongly disagree". Each category was coded from 1 to 5, depending upon the nature of the scale to which the statement contributed. For example, the difficulty scale was comprised of 14 statements which expressed opinions on the relative ease or difficulty of mathematics. Strong agreement with statements concerning the ease of mathematics were coded as 1, strong disagreement as 5. The reverse procedure was followed with statements concerning its difficulty. In a similar manner, strong agreement with positive statements concerning utility and enjoyment was coded as 5, whereas strong disagreement was coded as 1. Expressions of uncertainty were given a neutral value of 3. These values were summed according to the scale to which each statement contributed. As a result, a high score on each of the scales represented a strong tendency to perceive mathematics as difficult, enjoyable or useful.

5.12 Four statements which had been found to be statistically unrelated to the scales were analysed separately and did not contribute to the scales. Responses to three of the remaining 30 statements were found to correlate highly with both the utility and the difficulty scales and were treated as contributing to both scales. Responses to one other statement contributed to both the utility and the enjoyment scales.

5.13 The difficulty scale which appeared in the survey questionnaire consisted of 14 statements, with a possible range of scores from 14 to 70. The actual range was between 17 and 66, with a mean score of 40.4 (standard deviation: 10.2). High scores denoted a tendency to find mathematics a difficult subject. The statement "A lot of topics we study in maths make no sense to me", was most highly correlated with the total scale score (0.69). It would appear that this statement most clearly indicated the general sentiment of the scale.

5.14 The utility scale was based on 11 items, with a possible range of 11 to 55. The actual range was from 17 to 55, with a high score signifying that pupils agreed that mathematics was a useful subject. The mean of the sample was 38.1 (standard deviation: 7.5). Scores on the utility and difficulty scales were highly correlated, undoubtedly reflecting the fact that three statements were common to both scales. One of these statements, "I'm not interested in anything in maths but simple everyday arithmetic" was most highly correlated to the total utility item score. That it is also related to other statements reflecting difficulty with mathematics suggests the pervasive influence of perceived difficulty on other aspects of attitude toward mathematics. Other statements which expressed opinions concerning the use of mathematics outside of the school environment showed smaller correlations with the total score, suggesting that the scale itself reflected a more limited view of utility than is sometimes reported. This, in part, was the result of a deliberate effort to retain only those statements that evoked a range of response from pupils. The pilot indicated that statements referring to the more general usefulness of mathematics in life tended to elicit almost uniform agreement. It was only when a more personal view was presented that pupils differed in their assessment.

5.15 The enjoyment scale consisted of 9 statements. With a possible range of 9 to 45, the actual range was from 10 to 45, with a mean of 26.9 (standard deviation: 6.5). The statement that was most highly correlated with the total score was, "I enjoy working on maths problems", with which approximately 51 per cent of the pupils agreed.

5.16 All three scales showed a high degree of internal consistency (i.e. ranging from 0.80 to 0.88) indicating that the statements were reflecting a cohesive aspect of attitude toward mathematics.

Differences between girls and boys

5.17 One of the criteria for including a statement in a scale was that it evoked a range of responses that was approximately normally distributed. That the mean scores of the sample are close to mid-point of the possible range of scores is, therefore, not surprising. The mean of all the pupils' scores on a particular scale is determined by the construction of the scale, to the extent that a different set of statements could elicit more or less agreement or disagreement.

[1] *Investigation into the attitudes toward mathematics of some Sheffield school children.* Preece, M. and Sturgeon, S. Paper presented at 1980 annual conference of the British Educational Research Association, Cardiff, September 1980. 'Sex differences in mathematics achievement – a longitudinal study.' Hilton, T. and Berglund, G. *Journal of Educational Research,* 67, 1974, 5. *Encouraging Girls in Mathematics: the Problem and the Solution,* Brush, L., Cambridge, MA: Abt: Associates Press, 1980.

5.18 The scores themselves, therefore, have little meaning in an absolute sense and cannot be compared with those obtained from other surveys using other scales. However, they do have value for comparison purposes within the sample and in their relationship to other variables. In this regard, it is interesting that there were significant differences between boys' and girls' mean scores on all three scales. Girls found mathematics more difficult than boys (mean scores of 42.2, standard deviation: 10.1 versus 38.8, standard deviation: 10.1). They also enjoyed maths less (mean scores of 26.0, standard deviation: 6.4 versus 27.8, standard deviation: 6.5) and perceived it as less useful (mean scores 37.4, standard deviation: 7.8 versus 38.7, standard deviation: 7.3). However, the sex related differences in the latter 2 scales were small. Although statistically significant and consistent with the results of other studies which have compared boys and girls using similar measures, their educational significance is less clear than in the case of difficulty[1].

5.19 The differences in attitude between boys and girls was greatest in response to the difficulty scale and can be accounted for by a general tendency on the part of girls to agree with statements expressing a negative attitude. Although in the case of some statements the difference between the sexes was small, the discrepancy in response to a third of the statements on the difficulty scale was large enough to be considered statistically significant. For example, significantly more girls than boys believed that they had difficulty in remembering formulae, in understanding mathematical topics, and in applying the work that had been studied in class. (See Table 5.1). Almost 20 per cent more girls than boys considered themselves lucky if they did well on a maths test. On a more general level, only 10 per cent of the girls (as opposed to 25 per cent of boys) concurred with the statement "Maths is easy for me". It appears that difficulty is a pervasive factor in attitudes to mathematics and this is particularly true in the case of girls.

Table 5.1 *Statements to which there were significant differences in response pattern of girls and boys.*

Percentages of total sample responding to each category are given. The percentages of pupils who gave no response to individual statements are not included in the table but may be inferred from the discrepancies in total percentage.

		Strongly agree	Agree	Undecided	Disagree	Strongly disagree
Difficulty scale						
When it comes to doing a maths problem,	Boys	6	30	15	39	8
I get all the formulae mixed up.	Girls	8	42	14	29	3
When I do well on a maths test, I consider	Boys	5	25	7	41	20
myself lucky.	Girls	12	37	8	35	6
I can do the work in class but I don't	Boys	3	30	17	45	5
know how to apply it.	Girls	7	37	21	32	2
*Maths is easy for me.	Boys	5	20	17	40	16
	Girls	1	9	14	46	29
A lot of topics we study in maths make no	Boys	5	24	8	50	12
sense to me.	Girls	8	32	7	43	9
Enjoyment scale						
If you're a careful worker you'll find	Boys	14	46	8	26	6
maths easy enough.	Girls	9	38	8	35	6
Utility scale						
You won't be able to get on in life	Boys	20	43	7	22	7
without a good knowledge of maths.	Girls	18	34	9	30	6
I don't see the value of most of the maths	Boys	5	32	8	42	12
we do.	Girls	8	38	10	37	7
Other						
When you're thinking of a career, maths	Boys	7	17	14	38	22
is more important for boys than for girls.	Girls	4	15	6	38	35

*Also on Enjoyment scale.

5.20 In contrast, responses to statements on the enjoyment scale showed fewer and smaller differences between the sexes. Of the two statements that did evoke differences that were large enough to be considered significant, one has been noted previously. "Maths is easy for me" has been found to correlate equally highly with both the enjoyment and difficulty factors and contributed to both scales. On face value, the other statement "If you are a careful worker, you'll find maths easy enough" appeared to be concerned with difficulty, although it was clearly associated with the enjoyment factor and was considered as part of that scale. 13 per cent more boys than girls agreed with this statement, yielding a discrepancy in size of response that was comparable to those found in the difficulty scale. Other statements, more ostensibly related to interest and enjoyment in mathematical activities, evoked smaller differences.

5.21 Two statements from the utility scale also yielded significant differences between the sexes. More boys than girls agreed that a good knowledge of mathematics was necessary in order to get on in life and appeared to see the value of most of the work done in schools. Boys were also more inclined to see relevance in their mathematical education. For example, 11 per cent more boys than girls agreed that one would not be able to get along in life without a good knowledge of maths, while 9 per cent more girls did not see the value of much of the maths taught in schools. On the other hand, despite these sex differences in response, few girls agreed with the statement "When you're thinking of a career, maths is more important for boys than girls". Seventy three per cent of the girls, as compared with 60 per cent of the boys disagreed with the sentiments expressed in this statement. It seems that, when confronted with an opinion that is explicitly sex biased, girls are more likely to object, despite their relatively weaker endorsement of other statements concerning the usefulness of maths.

[1] *Nice girls don't study mathematics,* Boswell, S. and Katz, P. Report to the US National Institute of Education. 1980.

5.22 Furthermore, girls' disagreement with the statement was significantly associated with high scores on the item part of the questionnaire. In the case of boys, there was no relationship. This finding is in accord with others suggesting that sex stereotyping is related to poor performance on the part of girls[1].

Comparisons between primary and secondary

5.23 Because of the age difference between pupils in the primary and secondary surveys, different attitude scales were used in the two surveys and no general comparisons can be made. However, both scales did contain a common core of statements that, although not identical in wording, expressed the same opinion. Table 5.2 gives these statements and the pattern of responses to them among primary and secondary pupils. Since the primary survey had only three response categories (agree, disagree, uncertain), secondary pupils' positive responses were aggregated, as were their negative responses. This allowed for direct comparisons between the two groups.

5.24 Only one statement was common to the difficulty scales that appeared in both surveys. This statement was a general one, asserting that maths was easy (Set 1). It had evoked a large degree of uncertainty among primary pupils, with 45 per cent indicating that they were "not sure". In the secondary sample, pupils appeared to be more decisive. Although the proportion of boys who agreed with the statement remained constant at approximately 25 per cent, far fewer pupils were uncertain of their response and far more disagreed or strongly disagreed that "maths is easy for me". This shift to a negative position was exaggerated in the case of girls. Whereas at primary level the same proportion of girls and boys asserted that they found maths an easy subject, at secondary level, there was a drop of 10 per cent in the percentage of girls who agreed with the statement and a rise of over 40 per cent in the percentage of girls who disagreed. This shift to a negative attitude on the part of many pupils was also evident in response to two of the statements in the utility scale. At the primary level, the vast majority of

Table 5.2 *Percentage of responses to similar statements in the primary and secondary surveys.*

			Agree	Disagree	Uncertain
Set 1.					
Primary	I find maths an easy subject.	Boys	22	34	42
		Girls	20	34	46
Secondary	Maths is easy for me.	Boys	25	56	17
		Girls	10	75	14
Set 2.					
Primary	I think it's difficult to get on in life if you don't have much maths.	Boys	85	5	10
		Girls	86	7	7
Secondary	You won't be able to get on in life without a good knowledge of maths.	Boys	63	29	7
		Girls	52	36	9
Set 3.					
Primary	I don't need maths much outside of school.	Boys	20	61	19
		Girls	14	62	24
Secondary	I don't find much use for maths outside of school.	Boys	23	69	7
		Girls	28	65	4
Set 4.					
Primary	A lot of maths we do is a waste of time.	Boys	11	79	11
		Girls	7	80	13
Secondary	I don't see the value of most of the maths we do.	Boys	37	54	8
		Girls	46	44	10
Set 5.					
Primary	I enjoy everything we do in maths.	Boys	26	44	31
		Girls	32	38	31
Secondary	I find maths lessons interesting, whatever we are doing.	Boys	32	55	11
		Girls	33	53	11
Set 6.					
Primary	I like it when there is something new to learn in maths.	Boys	77	8	15
		Girls	75	9	16
Secondary	I enjoy the fact that there's something new to learn in maths.	Boys	66	24	9
		Girls	57	29	11

pupils (over 85 per cent) acknowledged the importance of mathematics to "getting on in life" (Set 2). However, this general affirmation was not apparent among 15 year olds. Although over half of the secondary pupils agreed, the proportion of pupils who disagreed rose by 24 per cent in the case of boys and 29 per cent in the case of girls. Again, the difference in response between boys and girls was statistically significant. It appears that 15 year old pupils, particularly girls, perceive maths as less important than do younger pupils.

5.25 On the other hand, "getting on in life" is of an immediate concern to most 15 year olds while, to the 11 year old, it is still a future event. Although similar, the two statements may be interpreted differently by the two age groups. That this may be the case is suggested by a comparison of responses to Sets 2 and 3. Whereas the same proportion of older pupils held similar attitudes to both statements, they evoked very different responses at the primary level. It appears that 11 year old pupils reacted differently to statements concerning their future career and to those concerning their present life and had seen a greater relevance of maths in the future, as contrasted to the present.

5.26 The third set of utility scale statements referred to the usefulness of mathematics in more specific terms, in reference to the topics taught in schools (Set 4). Whereas only 9 per cent of the primary age pupils agreed that a lot of maths was a waste of time, 37 per cent of secondary school boys and 46 per cent of the girls saw no value in most of the maths taught in school. The strength of the negative attitudes expressed in regard to the utility of the school curriculum is higher than that expressed to more general statements concerning the relevance of maths.

5.27 Two sets of statements on the enjoyment scales were common to both surveys. Although there were differences between younger and older pupils in their response patterns, these were generally not as great as those found in response to statements concerning difficulty or utility. For example, the larger number of pupils agreeing or disagreeing with Set 5 can be accounted for by the greater degree of certainty on the part of older pupils. Nevertheless, the increase in negative responses was greater than that shown to positive ones, confirming the general trend found among the other statements. Responses to Set 6 followed a similar pattern, although there was a significant difference in response between girls and boys.

5.28 Over the six sets of statements that were common to the two surveys, the greatest changes occurred in response to those referring to the difficulty and usefulness of maths. Almost without exception, the changes were in a negative direction, and these were particularly dramatic in the case of girls. In terms of difficulty, girls' responses shifted from a relatively neutral position at primary school age to a strongly negative one at 15 years old. This is the most extreme example, but girls' attitudes also changed substantially and to a significantly greater extent than boys in relation to the value of mathematics studied in school and the relevance of mathematics to "getting on in life".

Judgements of mathematical topics

Description

5.29 Pupils' attitudes to specific topics which form a part of the secondary school curriculum were investigated in two sections of the questionnaire. One section required them to rate a list of 17 topic names and mathematical activities in terms of interest and utility. Pupils were asked to respond to two scales (very interesting, fairly interesting, not interesting; and, very useful, fairly useful, not useful) for each item.

5.30 In the second section pupils were presented with 15 items from the written tests. These items were chosen to represent a range of the curriculum framework and were distributed in the following manner:

Main content category	*Number of items*
Number	5
Measures	5
Algebra	3
Geometry	2

5.31 Each item was of median facility in the sub-category from which it was chosen. Although in most cases this meant a facility of approximately 50 per cent, certain items (e.g. one involving matrices) were below this figure, while others were above it.

5.32 Pupils were requested to complete each item to the best of their ability and to mark "this type of problem" in terms of difficulty, interest and usefulness. Each of these dimensions was represented by a 5 point scale ranging from very easy to very difficult, very interesting to very boring, and very useful to useless. In order to conform with the general scales, higher ratings for difficulty, interest and utility were coded as 5, low ratings as 1. Pupils were also given the opportunity to explain the reasons for their ratings by adding comments in a space provided. If the item represented a topic which had not been covered in their school work, pupils were asked to indicate this.

[1] The frequencies in each response category to the two forms were compared using the Chi Square statistic.

5.33 Items of median facility had been chosen in order to minimise the effect of specific item difficulty on the subsequent ratings. It was intended that the items be seen as exemplars of a mathematical topic rather than as entities in themselves. In order to confirm that pupils' responses were, as instructed, to "this *type* of problem", comparisons were made between their ratings of the items and their ratings of the topic names which the items were assumed to represent. This could be done in the case of eight items which had been chosen as an exemplar of a topic or mathematical activity listed in the previous section. The resulting analysis[1] indicated a comparable response to the topic, whether it was embedded in a specific context or appeared as a general term.

5.34 In general, the analysis appeared to support the assumption that pupils' judgement of "this type of problem" were not limited to the specific item but may be generalised to the topic which the item represented.

Response to topic names

5.35 Among the 17 mathematical topics, activities involving computational skills were rated as the most useful. Over 50 per cent of the pupils rated long multiplication and calculation with decimals as very useful. Percentages dropped to 15 per cent or below in response to sets, facts about geometric shapes and working out algebraic expressions. In general, ratings for interest tended to be lower than those for utility. Long multiplication and equations elicited the largest proportion of positive responses with 27 per cent of the pupils believing that these activities were "very interesting".

5.36 Sex differences were observed, particularly in terms of usefulness, and, over the list as a whole, boys found the activities more interesting and more useful than did girls. These differences were significant in response to the geometric and measurement topics and continued the trend found in the primary survey indicating that boys liked these topics. It appears that preference in regard to these activities is established by 11 year olds and tends to remain stable throughout secondary schooling. Girls also maintained their early preferences. Although both sexes found long multiplication and decimals the most useful of the activities presented, at least 10 per cent more girls than boys indicated that they found them "very useful". Among the more advanced topics, girls found using logarithms very interesting, as opposed to a greater proportion of boys who indicated their interest in using formulae.

Response to items

5.37 Since some items had several parts, the possible range of scores on the 15 items was 0 to 21. Facilities on the individual items were similar to those obtained from the written tests, and the actual mean score achieved by the sample was 10.2 (standard deviation: 6.1).

5.38 In the case of every topic, there were pupils who indicated that they had not done "this type of problem" previously. The percentage ranged from 2 per cent in response to the computation of fractions to 33 per cent in response to an item involving matrices. Although these responses may, in some cases, have reflected the curriculum as taught (as may be true of the 22 per cent who indicated unfamiliarity with trigonometry), there is some indication that pupils may have been referring to the form of the item rather than its content. For example, when asked for the largest number that can be made by multiplying a two digit number by a one digit number, 18 per cent expressed unfamiliarity with this kind of problem. On the other hand, the 17 per cent who stated that they had not previously encountered the drawing of simple nets may have forgotten such work.

5.39 Although success in completing the items correctly was strongly related to pupils' regarding "this type of problem" as easy, some discrepancies did occur between perceived and actual difficulty as, for example, when fractional computation was presented in two contexts. One item, requiring the multiplication of 2 simple fractions, assessed computational skills only. The other required pupils to apply their skill in the solution of a verbal problem. The percentage of correct response for each was approximately 50 per cent, indicating that actual difficulty was comparable. However, whereas 64 per cent of the pupils rated the computation items as easy or very easy, only 30 per cent did so in response to the verbal problem involving the use of fractions. It appears that pupils perceive certain types of items as more difficult than their actual success rate would warrant.

5.40 Success in completing the items correctly did not appear to influence pupils' judgements with regard to interest or utility. For example, place value was considered to be one of the easiest of the topics presented (with 13 per cent more pupils indicating easy or very easy than were correct in answering the actual example). Conversely, it was considered to be one of the least interesting topics by the pupils, with almost 50 per cent stating that it was either not interesting or boring. A typical comment was *"This strikes me as pointless, except in a maths exam"*.

5.41 When each of the 15 topics was ranked in order of interest, utility and difficulty, the resulting analysis confirmed the strong relationship between pupils' judgements of a topic as useful and interesting. (See Table 5.3). Although these measures of association do not imply causation, it is not unlikely that the degree of interest that pupils find in topics is contingent upon their perception of its usefulness in their lives.

Table 5.3 *Rank order correlations between judgements of item/topics as interesting, useful and easy.*

	Interesting	Useful	Easy
Interesting	—	0.90	0.51
Useful		—	0.48
Easy			—

Differences between boys and girls

5.42 Boys' mean scores on the items (10.9, standard deviation: 6.0) were significantly higher than that of girls' (9.9, standard deviation: 6.1) and boys also showed a significantly greater tendency to judge topics as easy or very easy. However, even when the disparity between the relative performance of boys and girls was held constant, there was a significant overall difference in how difficult each sex believed the topics to be. As a general rule, boys perceived the topics to be less difficult than their success rate would warrant; whereas girls perceived the topics as more difficult.

5.43 Boys were significantly more successful than girls on 6 of the 15 items. In each of these cases a larger proportion of boys (as much as 24 per cent) found "this type of problem" easy. Overall, there was little difference in the judgement of item/topics as interesting or useful. However, on a specific level, boys found area and volume more interesting and useful than girls. They also found the verbal problem involving fractions more interesting and trigonometry more useful. With the exception of angles, those items which showed little difference in success rate elicited no difference in judgements.

5.44 The different response pattern between boys and girls is particularly evident in the examples which follow.

Example 1

[A diagram of an isosceles triangle with the two equal sides marked, and the bottom-right interior angle labelled 70°]

Calculate the other two interior angles of this isosceles triangle and write them in the diagram.

Percentage of responses in each category

	Easy/ very easy	Hard/ very hard	Correct	Incorrect	Omitted	Discrepancy per cent easy/very easy minus per cent correct
boys	66	21	65	23	12	1
girls	49	33	59	20	21	−10

5.45 Although more boys than girls gave the correct response to this item involving the calculations of angles, there were also more boys than girls who gave an *incorrect* response. This is partially accounted for by the fact that 9 per cent more girls omitted the item. When only the responses of those who actually attempted the item were compared, the percentage of correct responses was virtually identical for the two sexes. Boys' higher rate of response may be explained by their greater tendency to judge "this type of problem" as easy, interesting and useful. In their response, boys' perceptions of the relative difficulty coincided with their degree of success, whereas girls believed it to be more difficult than their success rate would indicate. This factor of "perceived difficulty" may have deterred girls from attempting the question.

Example 2

What is the largest number that can be made by multiplying a two digit number by a one digit number?

Percentage of responses in each category

	Easy/ very easy	Hard/ very hard	Correct	Incorrect	Omitted	Discrepancy per cent easy/very easy minus per cent correct
boys	65	17	55	27	17	10
girls	45	27	48	22	30	−3

5.46 A similar pattern emerged in response to the item assessing number concepts. Significantly more girls believed "this type of problem" was difficult and more stated that they had not done it before. As in the case of the angles item, those girls who did attempt to respond achieved the same success rate as boys (approximately 68 per cent). The difference between the sexes in percentage of correct response is not due to a greater degree of inaccuracy on the part of girls but to the fact that almost twice as many girls as boys did not attempt the item at all. On the other hand, there was no difference in the percentage of boys and girls who found it interesting or useful. Along with matrices and trigonometry, this type of question was considered to be the least interesting and useful of the set. As one pupil commented, *"I don't like this kind of problem because it seems pointless"*.

Example 3

$$\tfrac{1}{4} \times \tfrac{2}{3} = \ldots\ldots\ldots$$

Percentage of responses in each sub-category

	Easy/ very easy	Hard/ very hard	Correct	Incorrect	Omitted	Discrepancy per cent easy/very easy minus per cent correct
boys	67	21	47	44	9	20
girls	61	27	53	41	7	8

5.47 The above item was one of the two items which a larger proportion of girls than boys answered correctly. Both sexes tended to believe it to be easier than their success rate would warrant. However, the difference in the discrepancy is 20 per cent for boys, whereas it is 8 per cent for girls. Again, the degree of self-confidence shown by boys was greater than that shown by girls.

Relationships among attitude and performance measures

[1]'Attitudes toward mathematics', Aiken, L. in *Review of Educational Research*, 40, 1970, 551–596.

5.48 The questionnaire was concerned with two parallel but distinct concepts of "mathematics". One was mathematics in a general sense. It was assumed that pupils' reactions to statements referring to the usefulness, enjoyment and difficulty found in mathematics would yield valid measures of their feelings toward the term "mathematics". Although some of the statements referred to specific aspects of mathematics, none alluded to actual mathematical work done. Performance was not tested. Only beliefs, feelings and predispositions were involved. The second concept of mathematics was far more specific, focussing on the everyday aspects of the curriculum itself. It referred to the topics and skills that form "mathematics as taught" at the secondary school level. In order to reinforce the specificity and immediacy of this section, pupils were asked to *do*, as well as to *judge*. Although distinct, these two types of measures, directed at two different aspects of mathematics, were expected to be closely related. It was further assumed that the more specific measures would be more closely related to actual performance. However, the pattern of inter-relationship between attitude and performance was not obvious. Previous research suggested that the effect of attitude on performance is indirect and that performance level interacts with attitude in different ways[1]. Furthermore, it has been found that different aspects of attitude show differential influences on boys and girls. In order to explore these questions, the six attitudes measures were inter-correlated with attainment.

The measure of attainment was the pupils' raw scores on the written tests converted to a scaled performance score. (See Appendix 4.) The resulting correlations are presented in Table 5.4.

Table 5.4 *Intercorrelation between the attitude measures and performance score among boys (n = 474) and girls (n = 427).*

	General mathematics scales				Topic scales		
	Performance score	Enjoyment	Difficulty	Utility		Interest	Difficulty	Utility
Performance score	—	*15* 14	*−38* −44	*34* 30		*25** 09	*−61* −62	*40* 30
General enjoyment		—	*−58* −58	*56* 55		*48* 42	*−36* −31	*41* 38
General difficulty			—	*−72* −68		*−40** −27	*48* 53	*−42* −37
General utility				—		*44* 37	*−38* −36	*52* 46
Topic interest						—	*−39** −24	*62* 59
Topic difficulty							—	*−47* −44
Topic utility								—

Girls results in italic
Boys results in roman
*Significant difference between boys and girls

5.49 Over all the measures, the general difficulty and utility scales were most highly correlated. Partially, this is an artefact of the scales themselves in that they had three statements in common.

5.50 The performance score was most highly correlated with judgement of topics as more or less difficult. This is not surprising since the item exemplars were chosen from the larger set of items which determines this performance score. However, the fact that the correlation is not larger suggests that pupils' perception of difficulty is often at variance with their capability. This confirms the disparity noted between the proportion of students who judged "this type of problem" as easy against the proportion who were able to answer the example correctly.

5.51 Performance was also moderately related to a general difficulty scale and to both of the utility measures. It was essentially unrelated to the extent to which pupils found mathematics an enjoyable subject and to whether or not boys found topics interesting. In contrast, girls' interest in specific areas of mathematics showed a tendency to be related to their actual performance. This reflected a general trend. Overall, the correlations between the measures were higher for girls than for boys and significantly so in the case of three sets of variables. All these correlations involve the measure for interest. Whereas boys' performance was completely unrelated to whether or not they found a topic interesting, there was a significantly greater tendency for interest to be related to performance and to perception of difficulty on the part of girls. It appears that girls who find individual topics interesting are more apt to find them easy and to view mathematics as a less difficult subject. This relationship is less strong in the case of boys.

5.52 Although topic difficulty was highly correlated to actual performance on the tests, its relationships to topic utility and topic interest were of moderate magnitude. For boys, particularly, the difficulty of a topic had little effect on whether or not it was considered to be interesting. The perceived usefulness of a topic, on the other hand, was highly related to the extent of interest expressed by both girls and boys. The size of the correlation between the measures was similar to that found between topic difficulty and performance and confirms the rank order correlation between utility and interest (Table 5.3). If utility is taken to be the more objective of the measures, it may be argued that boys' and girls' interest in topics is contingent on the degree to which they find them useful in their lives.

The influence of performance

5.53 It has been suggested previously that the relationship between performance and attitudes is a reciprocal one of moderate but consistent magnitude. The correlations presented in Table 5.4 appear to confirm this. Although the levels of association between performance and measures of interest and enjoyment were low, those between performance and measures of utility and difficulty were moderate to high, confirming the findings of other research. However, such analysis gives no indication of the indirect influence that mathematical attainment may exert on the relationship among the attitude variables themselves. The possibility that performance may largely determine this relationship cannot be explored through a simple correlational analysis which is designed to give only the extent of association between two variables. The possibility that a third variable (for example performance) may be responsible for the apparent association can only be investigated by statistically removing its effect from the relationship. This procedure is called partial correlation analysis and is the statistical substitute for experimental controls. Essentially, a partial correlation between two variables is the correlation between two variables controlling for the effect of a third.

5.54 Table 5.5 presents the set of partial correlations between the attitude measures when the effect of performance was controlled. A comparison of these correlations with those presented in Table 5.4 indicates that actual performance did not affect the association between the enjoyment of mathematics and the other attitude measures. Regardless of their actual attainment, pupils who enjoyed mathematics generally tended to find it an easy and useful subject and judged the components of the curriculum as easy and useful.

Table 5.5   *Partial correlation coefficients between attitude measures with performance score controlled.*

	General mathematics scales			Topic scales		
	Enjoyment	Difficulty	Utility	Interest	Difficulty	Utility
General		−58	54	47	−34	39
enjoyment	—	−58	53	41	−28	36
General			−67	−34	33	−31
difficulty		—	−64	−26	37	−28
General				39	−23	45
utility			—	36	−24	41
Topic					−31	59
interest				—	−23	59
Topic						−31
difficulty					—	−33
Topic						
utility						—

Girls results in italic (n = 427)
Boys results in roman (n = 474)

5.55 Nor did performance have any effect on the close relationship between topic interest and topic utility. It appears that pupils view useful topics as interesting, regardless of their actual attainment on the mathematics tests.

5.56 On the other hand, performance did affect the association between topic difficulty and the other measures. In part, this is the result of the close relationship between performance and judgement of difficulty: i.e., those pupils who scored high on the written test generally tended to find specific topics easy; those who performed poorly judged individual topics as difficult. Nevertheless, even when the influence of performance scores was ruled out, there remained a moderate correlation between the topic difficulty and both the difficulty scale and topic utility.

5.57 Although the patterns of relationship among variables were comparable, actual performance exerted a smaller effect on boys' attitudes than on girls'. This was mainly due to the relatively stronger association between interest and performance on the part of girls.

The influence of utility

5.58 In order to explore the influence of utility on the relationships among the other variables, it was decided to examine the pattern of correlations that resulted when topic utility was held constant. The more specific measure of utility was chosen because of its greater relevance to the classroom and its high correlation with judgements of items as interesting. The procedure was similar to that which was used with the performance scores. The variance which each measure shared with topic utility was statistically removed from the scores and the transformed set of correlations was examined. (See Table 5.6). The partial correlations that resulted from the analysis indicate that topic utility accounted for the relationship between the general scales and the judgement of specific topics.

Table 5.6 *Partial correlation coefficients between attitude measures and performance score with topic utility scores controlled.*

	General mathematics scales				Topic scales	
	Performance	Enjoyment	Difficulty	Utility	Interest	Difficulty
Performance score	—	*02* 03	*−26* −37	*17* 19	*00* 11	*−52* −56
General enjoyment		—	*−50* −51	*44* 45	*32* 25	*−20* −17
General difficulty			—	*−64* −62	*−19* −07	*35* 44
General utility				—	*17* 14	*−18* −21
Topic interest					—	*−15* −03
Topic difficulty						—

Girls results in italic
Boys results in roman

5.59 While the inter-relationship of the scales which measured general attitudes toward mathematics remained high, with an average correlation of 0.5, the analysis confirms the earlier suggestion that interest in specific mathematical topics is strongly influenced by whether or not those topics are considered to be useful. Once these perceptions of utility had been accounted for, the relative ease or difficulty of a topic had little effect upon how interesting pupils found it. Furthermore, with topic utility removed, the relatively minimal relationship between actual performance and the measures of interest and enjoyment virtually disappeared. In the case of girls the association between performance and interest (see Table 5.4) can be explained entirely in terms of the strong relationship between interest and utility. It seems that whatever relationship exists between positive attitudes towards mathematics and performance is governed by how useful pupils see the topics they do, and this is particularly true of girls.

Sub-category scores and the attitude measures

5.60 As a final investigation of the relationship between performance and attitudes, the six attitude scales were correlated with pupils' performance on the individual curriculum sub-categories. Because of the written test design (3 sub-categories within each test) the number of pupils in the attitude subsample who were assessed on the same written test ranged from 127 to 231. These numbers were considered to be large enough for meaningful comparisons to be made. Table 5.7 gives the results of correlating written test scores and attitude measures

Table 5.7 *Written test scores and attitude measures*

| | | Scales | | | Topics | | |
		Enjoyment	Difficulty	Utility	Interest	Difficulty	Utility
Number	Concepts	*11*	*38*	*38*	*37*	*70*	*46*
		11	25	25	10	58	22
	Skills	*02*	*26*	*24*	*35*	*57*	*32*
		33	54	38	26	69	36
	Applications	*10*	*40*	*28*	*23*	*70*	*46*
		15	46	25	06	73	24
Measures	Unit	*25*	*42*	*28*	*55*	*67*	*61*
		05	34	15	03	66	02
	Rate and ratio	*12*	*19*	*23*	*16*	*43*	*09*
		17	49	35	26	52	32
	Mensuration	*09*	*25*	*21*	*21*	*58*	*18*
		04	44	29	12	56	52
Algebra	General	*15*	*50*	*42*	*29*	*69*	*39*
		24	48	30	01	56	30
	Traditional	*17*	*47*	*43*	*24*	*76*	*44*
		11	40	19	12	71	24
	Modern	*15*	*43*	*27*	*00*	*44*	*10*
		22	28	27	22	34	27
	Graphical	*34*	*55*	*56*	*12*	*67*	*53*
		05	26	26	06	46	10
Geometry	Descriptive	*30*	*49*	*37*	*13*	*75*	*39*
		05	37	22	22	51	42
	Modern	*22*	*39*	*33*	*29*	*56*	*55*
		13	25	16	04	75	31
	Trigonometry	*27*	*21*	*26*	*22*	*61*	*45*
		23	47	34	15	43	25
Probability and Statistics	Probability	*29*	*49*	*49*	*44*	*52*	*22*
		17	38	17	12	50	19
	Statistics	*07*	*36*	*25*	*29*	*73*	*48*
		04	36	13	04	65	20

Girls results in italic
Boys results in roman

for boys and girls. Girls' results are given in italic and boys' results in roman type-face.

5.61 As was evident in Table 5.4, topic difficulty had the highest overall correlation with the sub-category scores. This more discriminating analysis indicated that performance on items involving number application and traditional algebra was highly related to whether or not pupils judged specific topics as difficult. In contrast, performance in modern algebra was only moderately related to judgements of difficulty.

5.62 In general, girls' performance on individual areas of the curriculum was more closely related to their attitude than was the case with boys. This is particularly evident in their perception of the relative utility of curriculum topics. The difference in the strength of the relationship between performance on unit measures and graphical algebra and on utility was most markedly different between the sexes. Whereas boys' attainment in these areas had little or no relationship to their overall judgement of topics as useful, girls' judgements and attainment were strongly related. Not only did girls who scored highly on these sub-categories tend to perceive the topics as useful, but they were likely to agree with statements expressing enjoyment in mathematics. Performance on unit measures was also strongly related to their finding topics interesting. Performance on graphical algebra and probability was also more strongly related to the attitude measures among girls. In contrast, among the set of sub-categories boys' performance on the number skills was seen to be more strongly related to their general attitudes towards mathematics.

Pupils' statements about mathematics

5.63 Before the pupils responded to the more structured sections of the questionnaire, they were presented with a series of questions about their attitudes towards school subjects in general and mathematics in particular. All but a few pupils answered these questions. Their responses, which are discussed below, are occasionally supplemented by those from the pilot interviews.

5.64 Initially pupils were asked to state their favourite school subject and to give the reasons for their choice. The following responses were given:

	%
General practical subjects (for example art, games, etc.)	33
English	12
Mathematics, including technical drawing, accounting and computer studies	11
Science (biology, physics, chemistry and general science)	17
History	7
Geography	5
Language (French, German, Spanish)	5
Religion, community, social and classical studies and sociology	3
Commerce and economics	2
Typing, shorthand, office practice	4
Other subjects	2

5.65 Some of the responses were, undoubtedly, influenced by the format of the courses which the pupils were currently studying. For example, some said that they liked History because of the topic work which they were engaged in, others that they liked English because of its emphasis on oral reports. However, more general patterns did emerge.

5.66 Pupils who gave English or History as their favourite subject often cited its relevance to their everyday lives. Pupils wrote:

"History is my favourite subject because it deals with people and things which really did exist."

"I like to find out about events in the past and how they influence current world situations."

"Books are part of our lives."

"You speak English every day."

5.67 Beyond this, those who preferred English appeared to see themselves as in control of their own work. They pointed to the fact that their opinions were valued, that they could use their own experiences, and that they could help themselves to succeed. They liked its variety and the fact that there was no set pattern of work. *"You are given a topic to write on or answer questions on, and you word and compose your own thoughts. You use your own views to compose."*

5.68 In contrast, mathematics appears for some pupils to be a rule-bound subject with approved methods leading to a single correct solution.

"Maths is rather boring and tedious. It deals with facts, logic and precise figures. It leaves nothing to the imagination, and is taught in school in a routine, boring way."

5.69 For others who preferred mathematics, its more formal, less personalised approach was often its attraction. These pupils disliked subjects in which grades seemed to depend upon opinions – either their own or those of the teacher. They were comforted by the fact that, in maths, there was a definite right or wrong answer. *"Everything fits together." "You know when you've finished the question."* These pupils tended to complain about the memory load in the Arts subjects and the problem of *"getting things down on paper."* For them maths was applying rules and working things out. They enjoyed the feeling that they had achieved something when they arrived at a correct solution, *"proving to yourself that you can do it".* Pupils wrote of the challenge of maths problems and their variety. During the interviews, one top stream girl expressed a view of maths as a creative enterprise in comparison with arts. She declared, *"Fact is fact, while in maths there are so many variations."*

Another stated, *"Unlike English, which we speak all the time, there are always completely new things in maths."*

5.70 That mathematics courses tend to be presented as a series of distinct topics was looked upon as an asset by some and as a liability by others. Those who enjoyed maths looked upon the lack of obvious cohesion in the maths topics as an opportunity for a fresh start each time. They enjoyed the fact that every new topic is new to everyone and looked upon it as a challenge.

5.71 To others, the procession of new topics led to confusion. Again and again pupils wrote of the difficulty in beginning a new topic. Others complained of the lack of time. A typical comment from such pupils was: *"We change from one topic to another without actually understanding the previous one, and then are expected to know all about it."*

5.72 Another problem associated with the topic approach in maths was the tendency to forget previously learned material.

"The hardest thing for me in maths is actually remembering what I have been taught, because you have to concentrate on the next topic and you forget a topic done a year or so ago."

"It takes me a long time before I am able to remember how to do certain problems and by the time I have done so we are beginning a new topic; therefore, I cannot put my ideas into practice."

5.73 The theme of boredom emerged on different levels. Although repetitive skill topics were considered tedious, boredom was often associated with lack of understanding.

"I think maths is alright when I can understand and do the thing but when I cannot do the thing I get bored and that puts me off maths."

"It is alright sometimes. It depends on what you are doing. It is boring if you don't know what the teacher is talking about."

"I like it if I can understand the work."

5.74 The problem of understanding appears to be a real and consistent one. The rationale for using certain methods was often unclear in pupils' minds, with the result that greater reliance was placed upon memory. Formula was most frequently cited as a source of difficulty. Although pupils wrote of the problem of memorising formulae, most went on to refer to the additional difficulty of relating the appropriate procedure to a particular problem. The confusion experienced by such pupils is summed up in the following statements:

"I have difficulty distinguishing between the questions and what methods are used on each question. Also remembering rules and formulas applying to each topic. I find it hard to read a question and know what rules, formulas, etc. to use."

"I have difficulty in understanding why a problem is worked out in a certain way."

5.75 Related to this was pupils' difficulty in knowing what was being asked of them, particularly in the case of verbal problems.

"The hardest thing in maths is knowing how to attack or break down a problem in simple terms and to solve a problem which involves many steps."

"It's hard to grasp the way to tackle a problem. Once I have got it I am alright."

And, more generally,

"The hardest thing about maths is knowing what to do and how to do it."

"The hardest thing about some topics in maths is that they don't have a reasonable amount of logic behind them so it is difficult to understand."

As one pupil suggested: *"It's not so much remembering as understanding."*

5.76 Compounding the problem of understanding is the additional problem of computational skills. There is no doubt that most pupils find involved computations tedious. However, computational errors are rarely obvious, and even the more successful admit that they tend to make careless mistakes. Although a pupil who is confident of his/her ability may realise that the reason for the error was a computational one, those less confident are less sure of the sources of the error. In an interview during the pilot study, one pupil described the situation,

"Your mind goes faster than your hand, so you tend to make silly mistakes and don't get the correct answer. Then you believe that it's your thinking that's wrong, not carelessness."

Others wrote:

"The hardest part is the very long complicated calculations where if you make a tiny mistake your answer is totally wrong. I find these very frustrating."

5.77 Others spoke of the inability to use maths books as a ready and easy reference, which inevitably leads to greater dependency on teacher help.

"I find revision of maths difficult. In my books all I have is a mass of answers which mean nothing to me. The text books do not offer good written explanations."

"I sometimes find the text book ambiguous which frustrates me – the questions in it are confusing and not always clear as to what they mean."

5.78 The practical importance of exam results received general agreement. Whether for this reason, or the nature of the subject, exams were cited as a major source of anxiety. The necessity for speed, in particular, was commented upon by pupils.

"When your exam comes, your mind goes blank. You can't remember the formulas you revised – especially if you revised. When you see other people getting on, you've got to rush for the time. You leave a question you can't do. When you go on, your mind is still thinking of the old question. You can't concentrate on the next one."

"They write down differently in the exam to what your teacher would put on the board. You think, I've never seen this before, and then I really work on what they're on about."

"You don't realise that what you are supposed to do is the same as what you've been taught."

5.79 To the question, "Do you think that people need maths to get on in life?", the answer was overwhelmingly affirmative. 90 per cent of pupils gave an unequivocal "Yes", 4 per cent more qualified their agreement. In explaining their position, there was a tendency to view a maths qualification as a passport to future work.

"Maths is one element you need in society as a whole because without a good maths exam CSE, GCE, you'll find it very hard to get a job."

"I wish I could get to like the subject, because it's so essential to a good career."

5.80 On the other hand, this pragmatic approach led many pupils to judge mathematical activities only in terms of their utility. Many resented the fact that the topics which they studied seemed irrelevant to their future careers.

"It is an obviously integral part of life but I feel that it covers a range of subjects which may never again be thought about. In short, I think much of maths is a waste of time."

"The mathematical theories are interesting but unfortunately not all of the topics have practical uses. For this reason, I find that in many topics I lose some incentive to work hard."

5.81 Asked about the topics which they considered the most useful, approximately 45 per cent mentioned the four operations or basic arithmetic. Another 17 per cent gave fractions, decimals or percentages. Money management topics, such as interest, income tax and banking procedures were also cited by over 10 per cent of the pupils.

5.82 When questioned about how they felt about topics that didn't seem useful, pupils responses covered a wide range of opinion from:

"I enjoy doing them and that is what really counts."

"I feel that if someone likes maths all topics are useful."

to:

"Unenthusiastic. They tend to take a lot of concentration and if I can't see the point of them my attention wanders.

"They are a complete waste of time. At this time in our education, when we need all the practice at the basic essentials, it is stupid doing something like that."

Conclusions and reference to other investigations

5.83 The survey has used a variety of measures to explore the range of perceptions and feelings that can be categorised as "attitudes toward maths". Although in no way replicating any previous investigations, it has confirmed much of the existing literature on adolescent attitudes. In addition, it has attempted to focus on some of the components of the curriculum which may be more amenable to change than generalised beliefs. The most significant findings to emerge from the investigation concern the effect of pupils' perceptions of the utility of mathematics on their attitudes towards it, the difference in attitudes between boys and girls and the change in attitudes as pupils progress through their school careers. Each of these findings will be discussed in turn.

(i)   The effect of pupils' perceptions of the utility of mathematics on their attitudes towards it.

[1]Preece, M and Sturgeon, S. op. cit.
'Adolescent attitudes toward maths', Callahan, W. in *The mathematics teacher,* LXIV, 1971, 8.
[2]Boswell, S. and Katz, P. op. cit.

5.84 The perception of mathematics as useful was found to be the most powerful of the attitude variables. This was particularly true in the case of the more specific measure of utility, the degree to which individual topics were seen to be useful. Interest in a topic was largely contingent upon its utility, whereas its relative ease or difficulty had little effect. Utility also, to varying degrees, accounted for the relationship between performance and the other attitude measures. This is consistent with the findings of other surveys. For example, when pupils have been asked to volunteer reasons for their liking mathematics, the most common response had been a reference to its utility[1]. Other researchers have suggested that with age the perception of mathematics as useful increases in importance as a predictor of mathematics achievement[2]. In this survey, utility showed a strong direct and indirect relationship with performance, and this was particularly so in the case of girls.

(ii)   The difference in attitude between boys and girls

5.85 It would be inaccurate to conclude that boys' attitudes toward mathematics were generally more positive than those of girls. Girls found specific mathematical topics as interesting and as useful as boys. Although they tended to look upon mathematics as less enjoyable and less useful a subject than did boys, the degree of difference was not great. The notable discrepancy in attitudes between the sexes occurred in their perception of the difficulty of mathematics, both generally and specifically.

5.86 In response to the attitude scales, girls showed a consistent tendency to agree or strongly agree with statements referring to difficulty or lack of competence. Although girls performed less well on the written test items in the questionnaire, there is evidence that their lack of confidence was not contingent upon their actual performance. For example, their response to the statement, "Maths is easy for me" was completely unrelated to their performance score, whereas in the case of boys there was a small but significant relationship between the two variables. Furthermore, the discrepancy between perceived difficulty of the topics and actual difficulty, as measured by correctness in answering the exemplar items, was significantly larger for boys than for girls. In general, boys judged topics as easier than their success rate would indicate, while girls judged them as more difficult.

[1]'Sex: A perspective on the attribution process.' Deaux, K., in *New directions in attribution theory research* (Vol. 1), J. H. Harvey, W. J. Ickes and R. F. Kidd (eds), Hillsdale, N. J.: Erlbaun, 1976.
[2]Preece and Sturgeon, op. cit.
'Sex-related differences in mathematics achievement, spatial visualisation and affective factors' Fennema, E. and Sherman, J. in *American educational research journal.* 14, 1977, 1.

[1]Fennema, E. and Sherman, J. op. cit.

5.87 These findings are consistent with more general research suggesting that males have a consistently higher level of expectation than do females. Deaux has stated, "One of the most pervasive findings in the literature on sex differences is the lower expectations which females hold for their performance as compared with males"[1]. With specific reference to mathematics, girls' lack of confidence in their mathematical ability has proved to be a consistent finding[2].

5.88 In a longitudinal study in the US, Fennema and Sherman[1] found that "At each grade level from 6 to 12, boys were significantly more confident in their abilities to deal with mathematics than were girls. In most instances, this happened when there were no significant sex-related differences in mathematics achievement." They go on to conclude: "It may be that stereotyping mathematics as a male subject is a mediating variable affecting a variety of relevant attitudes, for example, confidence and/or perception of the usefulness of mathematics".

[1]Boswell, S. and Katz, P. op. cit.

5.89 Although the survey did not explicitly investigate the reasons for girls' comparative lack of confidence, some of its findings do support the contention that girls' attitudes are affected by the perception of mathematics as a male subject. For example, although the majority of both boys and girls expressly denied that maths is more important in terms of career for boys than girls, response to this statement was significantly correlated to performance only in the case of girls. Lower achieving girls tended to agree with the statement, whereas high achievers disagreed. This confirms a similar finding in the US that "among girls the higher the level of stereotyping, the lower the achievement score"[1]. It also indirectly supports the finding of Preece and Sturgeon of a significant negative correlation among girls between liking maths and viewing it as a male domain.

[1]Aiken, L. op. cit.
Fennema, E. and
Sherman, J. ibid.
[1]'Some speculations and
findings concerning sex
differences in mathematical
abilities and attitudes,'
Aiken, L. Jr. in
*Mathematics learning: what
research says about sex
differences,* Fennema, E.
(ed.), Columbus, Ohio:
ERIC, 1975.
'The relationship between a
seventh-grade pupil's
academic self-concept and
achievement in mathematics,'
Bachman, A. in *Journal for
research in mathematics
education,* 1, 70, 173–179.
[2]'Differences between the
sexes in mathematics and
science courses.' Keeves, J.
in *International review of
education,* 19, 1973, 1, 47–62.
Fox, L., Brody, L., and
Tobin, D.
[3]*A national assessment of
achievement and participation
of women in mathematics.*
Report to U.S. National
Institute of Education 1979.

5.90 More suggestive is the sex discrepancy in response to "When I do well in a maths test, I consider myself lucky", a statement which was agreed to by significantly more girls than boys. This accords with research indicating that attributions made by males and females for their own performance show distinct differences. It has been found that men are more likely to claim ability as the cause of success whereas the woman who succeeds, particularly at that which is considered as a masculine task, is more likely to attribute success to luck. Although the discrepancy cited above is in response to a single statement, it does accord with the observation that both men and women are more likely to perceive mathematics as a male domain[1].

5.91 Both attitudes in general and self-confidence in particular have been found to be more clearly related to the performance of girls than to that of boys[1]. Furthermore, whereas high achieving girls have been observed to have many of the same interests and attitudes toward mathematics as their male counterparts[2], sex differences tend to occur among those of middle and lower attainment. These girls have been found to be particularly vulnerable to lack of confidence[3].

(iii) Age differences

[1]Preece and Sturgeon, op.cit.
Hilton, T. and Berglund, G.
op. cit.
Brush, L. op. cit.
'A longitudinal study in
mathematics attitude,'
Anthonen, R. in *Journal
of Educational Research,*
62, 1969, 10, 467–471.

5.92 Because of the substantial age difference between the two groups, primary and secondary pupils were not given the same attitude scales. However, a comparison of responses to similar statements in both surveys indicates that pupils find mathematics more difficult, less useful and less enjoyable as they grow older. This confirms other research that has charted the decline of positive attitudes towards mathematics as pupils progress through their schooling[1]. Particularly interesting is the change in perception of the utility of mathematics. Whereas, at 11 years old, pupils believe that mathematics will play an important part in their future careers, at 15 years many more pupils are dubious about its relevance to their everyday life. Partially, this may reflect the fact that "getting on in life" is theoretical for most 11 year olds as opposed to 15 year olds. On the other hand, it may be a reaction to more specific components of the curriculum. At 15, pupils may have a different perception of what constitutes "mathematics", and, consequently, a less positive attitude towards it.

6 The survey results

The pattern of results

[1] *Mathematical development. Secondary survey report No.1.* HMSO, 1980, Price £6.60.

6.1 The pattern of results obtained in the 1979 survey was similar to that described in the first secondary survey report[1]. This similarity in the general picture applied to mathematics as a whole and also within the bands of the background variables (proportion of pupils taking free school meals, pupil/teacher ratio, size of age group, location, region and sex of pupil).

[1] Op. cit. Chapter 6, p. 119

6.2 This second secondary report has therefore focussed on the results obtained in certain selected areas of the mathematics curriculum. The more detailed examination of the results in these areas relates to a statement made in the concluding chapter of the second secondary survey report[1]: "The facility value of an individual item does not reveal which of its characteristics have influenced that facility." This report details a number of ways in which the relationships between item characteristics and pupil responses have been investigated: for example in both the written and the practical tests, more detailed coding schemes were used than in the 1978 survey; in the written tests the responses made to items of related content were contrasted; and in the practical tests separate coding schemes were used to record pupils' answers to questions and the methods they used to obtain their answers.

6.3 It is, however, a matter for informed judgement and investigation by teachers and researchers to determine the reasons for any relationships suggested by the results obtained.

Summary

6.4 This report has added detail to the picture relating to a number of mathematical topics. The practical assessment (Chapter 2) showed that 60 per cent or more of the pupils could use a protractor, a ruler and a balance for a basic measuring task. Concepts related to these measures were not so well understood. Calculators were familiar to nearly all the pupils: only a few were unable to use them to do a one-operation calculation and over 80 per cent could use them to do a two-operation calculation. Means of checking answers, however, were known by about 50 per cent fewer in each case and complex calculations revealed that many pupils had difficulties with understanding notation and number operations.

6.5 The results of the written tests reported in Chapter 3 related to five item clusters: numeration, number operations, ratio, symbolic representation and angles. These results suggested that concepts such as algebraic notation and angles were understood at an elementary level by over half the pupils and place value by three-quarters. Several features of the data indicated that many pupils had a fragile grasp of these concepts: for example, results showed the extent to which extraneous factors can influence judgements of angle size; and a steep rise in the incidence of errors in algebraic representation in relation to the number of abstract symbols used and the familiarity of the setting was also noted.

6.6 In several instances the errors made by the 15 year olds in the written and practical tests were compared with those made by 11 year old pupils in response to the same or similar items. For example, when asked to compare decimal numbers less than one almost as many 15 year olds as 11 year olds (over 20 per cent) appeared to ignore decimal points. In the practical topic on fractions about 70 per cent of the secondary pupils gave the correct response to the item $\frac{1}{2} + \frac{1}{4}$ compared to about 60 per cent of the 11 year olds in their written test survey. However, the proportion of older pupils adding numerators and denominators to obtain the answer $\frac{2}{6}$ was, at 10 per cent, nearly as high as that of the 11 year olds (13 per cent).

6.7 In relation to the concept of angle some 20 per cent of 15 year olds compared to about one-third of 11 year olds judged angle size on the basis of an irrelevant feature such as the size of the arc labelling the angle. The incidence of errors in algebraic notation varied with context and with the symbols used. In the specific instance of substituting the value of a variable raised to a power, around 20 per cent of 15 year olds employed the index as a multiplying factor; about 50 per cent of 11 year olds made this type of error.

6.8 Pupils' attitudes to mathematics in general and to mathematical topics were surveyed for the first time at secondary level. Attitudes to mathematics generally were measured on three scales relating to enjoyment, difficulty and usefulness of mathematics. The perceived usefulness of mathematics proved to be the most influential of these variables, especially in relation to individual topics, and particularly so in the case of girls. However, girls differed most from boys in their perception of mathematics as difficult: there was evidence that boys tended to underrate the difficulty of mathematical exercises in relation to their performance and girls to overrate it.

Developments in the monitoring programme

6.9 Development of existing assessment procedures is continuing and new assessment materials are being piloted. At present the major area of item development is problems, applications, and investigations. Trials of some written test items in this area have taken place and further materials are being piloted using ideas produced in association with groups of teachers. Tests called "patterns and problems" are also being developed for inclusion in the 1981 monitoring surveys onwards. The written tests taken by the main sample are now to be known as "concepts and skills" to distinguish them from the new materials.

6.10 Practical mathematics topics concerned with patterns and problems are also being developed and have been included in the secondary surveys since 1980. In the first two surveys the focus in the practical tests was on pupils' understanding of certain concepts and their performance in skills of measuring and calculating. The aim now is to include in all topic areas a situation which requires more than the exercise of a skill or the remembering of a rule. Other topics explore pupils' awareness of patterns and the extent to which they can generalise.

6.11 In relation to pupils' attitudes to mathematics, the development includes the piloting of a procedure for investigating pupils' preferences for types of presentation of mathematical material. A structured interview is also under consideration.

6.12 The items in the written tests of concepts and skills, taken by all pupils in the sample, are split into 15 sub-categories of content. In several of these sub-categories the detail of pupils' performance can only be sketchy because of limitations in the number of test items. As from 1980, however, the surveys are being designed in such a way that more detailed coverage can be given to particular sub-categories. In order to compensate for the increased coverage in these areas, other areas are being temporarily omitted or reduced.

6.13 The report on the 1980 secondary survey will contain some more extensive discussion of the work on patterns and problems and will also provide some results from those sub-categories which were given increased coverage.

Appendix 1

The survey sample

1.1 The sampling strategy adopted for this second survey of 15 year old pupils' performance in mathematics was very similar to that used for the first. Full details are given in the report of that survey. In deciding on the sampling strategy, a balance has been struck between the need for a sample large enough to allow useful inferences concerning the national population to be drawn and the need to avoid overburdening either schools or individual pupils.

1.2 A two-stage sampling procedure was used in which a stratified sample of schools was drawn first and a sample of pupils chosen from each selected school by reference to their dates of birth. The proportion of pupils selected from each sample school varied according to the size of the 15-plus age group in the school (the larger the age group, the smaller the proportion of pupils sampled) since with this approach it is easier to predict the number of pupils who will be sampled at the second stage and more large schools are used, making it more likely that a representative sample of these schools will be obtained.

1.3 Since only a sample of the pupils in each school is tested, the two-stage sampling procedure demonstrates the Assessment of Performance Unit's declared intention of monitoring performance nationally and not concerning itself with the performance of individual pupils or schools.

Impact on schools and pupils

1.4 Schools had the option of not participating and of withdrawing individual pupils from the testing if it was thought likely to cause them undue distress. Although large-scale withdrawals would have had serious consequences for both the representativeness and size of the achieved sample it was felt that schools should be allowed this discretion. The extent to which it was exercised in this survey can be seen in Table A1.1. The effect of participation in the survey upon individual pupils was minimised by giving only a small number of the available items to each pupil and by keeping the testing sessions fairly short.

Table A1.1

(a) The sample of schools

| | Number of schools | | | |
	England	Wales	N. Ireland	TOTAL
Invited to take part	618	62	76	756
Unable to take part	30	9	3	42
Did not reply	24	2	4	30
Pupil data form not returned or received too late*	15	—	2	17
Tests not received at NFER	14	—	2	16
Tests returned unused	1	1	—	2
Tests received	534	50	65	649

	England	Wales	N. Ireland	TOTAL
Practical				
Schools taking part	194	16	17	227
Attitudes				
Schools taking part	141	13	16	170

(b) The sample of pupils

	England	Wales	N. Ireland	TOTAL
Total sample	8,306	2,117	2,842	13,265
Absent	286	109	95	490
Withdrawn	19	5	4	28
Number completing tests	8,001	2,003	2,743	12,747

*See later account of procedure for preserving pupil anonymity.

The survey sample

[1]These dates correspond to the school year in England and Wales. In Northern Ireland, however, the school year runs from 2 July to 1 July the following year. This means that in Northern Ireland, approximately five-sixths of the sample were fifth year pupils and the remainder fourth year pupils.

[1]Schools with fewer than four pupils in the relevant age group were excluded for administrative reasons.

1.5 The target population was defined as all pupils born between 1 September 1963 and 31 August 1964, i.e. pupils whose sixteenth birthday fell between 1 September 1979 and 31 August 1980 inclusive[1]. Pupils in special schools or special units within schools were excluded.

1.6 it was intended to test approximately 10,000 pupils in England, and about 2,500 in each of Wales and Northern Ireland, i.e. about $1\frac{1}{2}$ per cent and 5 per cent of the age groups respectively. As described above, the proportion of pupils in the age group sampled in each school depended on the number of pupils in the 15-plus age group in the school, and the following proportions were used:

Size of 15+ age group	Proportion of age group tested (%)
4 – 80 pupils[1]	40
81 – 160 pupils	20
161 – 240 pupils	10
over 240 pupils	7

[1]Schools with fewer than four pupils in the relevant age group were excluded for administrative reasons.

1.7 In order to ensure that all regions of the country and all types and sizes of school were represented, the population of schools in England and Wales was stratified in four ways: by type of school, size of the 15-plus age group, by region and by location as shown below:

Type of school:	Comprehensive to age 16
	Comprehensive to age 18
	Other maintained
	Independent

Size of 15-plus age group	4 – 80 pupils[1]
	81 – 160 pupils
	161 – 240 pupils
	over 240 pupils

Region: North
                                       South
                                       Midlands
                                       Wales

Location: In metropolitan counties
                                       In non-metropolitan counties

Details of the local education authorities in each region and their designation as metropolitan or non-metropolitan are given in Table A1.2.

Table A1.2

Counties in regions of England and Wales

North	Midlands	South	Wales
Merseyside*	West Midlands*	Greater London*	Clwyd
Greater Manchester*	Hereford & Worcester	Bedfordshire	Dyfed
South Yorkshire*	Salop	Berkshire	Gwent
West Yorkshire*	Staffordshire	Buckinghamshire	Gwynedd
Tyne & Wear*	Warwickshire	East Sussex	Mid Glamorgan
Cleveland	Derbyshire	Essex	Powys
Cumbria	Leicestershire	Hampshire	South Glamorgan
Durham	Lincolnshire	Hertfordshire	West Glamorgan
Humberside	Northamptonshire	Isle of Wight	
Lancashire	Nottinghamshire	Kent	
North Yorkshire	Cambridgeshire	Oxfordshire	
Northumberland	Norfolk	Surrey	
Cheshire	Suffolk	West Sussex	
		Isle of Scilly	
		Avon	
		Cornwall	
		Devon	
		Dorset	
		Gloucestershire	
		Somerset	
		Wiltshire	

*Metropolitan Counties

Northern Ireland Education and Library Boards

Belfast
North Eastern
Southern
South Eastern
Western

1.8 The schools in Northern Ireland were stratified for sampling by the size of 15-plus age group:

4 – 80 pupils
81 – 160 pupils
161 – 240 pupils
over 240 pupils

The sample was then weighted to reflect the correct proportions of type of school according to the following categories:

Grammar controlled
Grammar other
Intermediate controlled
Intermediate other
Technical college

Table A1.3: *The obtained sample.*

Region & Location	Type	Size of age group	4–80		81–160		161–240		241+	
			Pupils	Schools	Pupils	Schools	Pupils	Schools	Pupils	Schools
NORTH — Non-Metropolitan / Metropolitan	Comprehensive to 16		0	0	139	9	237	18	38	2
	Comprehensive to 18		0	0	28	3	122	9	313	17
	Grammar/Sec. Modern		8	1	40	2	14	1	0	0
	Independent		40	3	16	1	0	0	0	0
	Comprehensive to 16		12	1	81	5	161	14	42	3
	Comprehensive to 18		0	0	85	5	314	24	586	33
	Grammar/Sec. Modern		28	2	179	11	54	4	31	2
	Independent		32	2	27	2	0	0	0	0
MIDLANDS — Non-Metropolitan / Metropolitan	Comprehensive to 16		59	3	72	6	153	11	73	5
	Comprehensive to 18		0	0	51	3	251	17	483	25
	Grammar/Sec. Modern		28	2	86	6	82	5	14	1
	Independent		53	4	76	4	0	0	0	0
	Comprehensive to 16		0	0	58	4	72	5	44	2
	Comprehensive to 18		0	0	43	4	118	10	122	7
	Grammar/Sec. Modern		0	0	0	0	0	0	0	0
	Independent		0	0	0	0	0	0	0	0
SOUTH — Non-Metropolitan / Metropolitan	Comprehensive to 16		0	0	107	8	256	19	201	13
	Comprehensive to 18		0	0	201	16	322	24	534	30
	Grammar/Sec. Modern		7	1	355	21	110	8	60	3
	Independent		174	16	97	6	25	2	0	0
	Comprehensive to 16		0	0	0	0	56	4	11	1
	Comprehensive to 18		19	2	57	4	340	28	240	15
	Grammar/Sec. Modern		0	0	25	2	53	4	0	0
	Independent		36	2	9	1	0	0	0	0
WALES	Comprehensive to 16		0	0	81	2	99	3	0	0
	Comprehensive to 18		31	1	588	13	441	12	384	9
	Grammar/Sec. Modern		108	3	0	0	0	0	0	0
	Independent		147	4	0	0	0	0	0	0
NORTHERN IRELAND	Grammar Controlled		60	1	142	3	43	1	0	0
	Grammar Other		141	3	211	5	24	1	0	0
	Intermediate Cont.		264	7	533	14	168	4	45	1
	Intermediate Other		144	4	636	13	0	0	0	0
	Technical College		102	3	159	4	48	1	0	0

Written tests

1.9 A sample of 756 schools was randomly selected within the stratification framework, and their headteachers contacted and asked if they, and their pupils, could take part in the survey. Table A1.1 gives details of the response rate achieved, with 649 schools providing data for the analyses described in this report.

1.10 The total sample of pupils for whom tests were sent to schools was 13,265 and after absences and withdrawals, the tests from 12,747 pupils were returned to the NFER for marking (Table A1.1). Some of these were rejected subsequently for various reasons, for example, faulty test booklets, answers illegible, etc. In the event, test scores from 12,459 pupils were included in the analyses described in this report.

Practical tests

1.11 A sub-sample was randomly selected for the practical testing from the schools and pupils taking the written tests. 27 testers visited 227 schools and tested approximately 1,150 pupils.

Attitude survey

1.12 A different sub-sample of approximately 1,000 pupils in 170 schools was randomly selected for the investigation of pupils' attitudes to mathematics.

Anonymity

1.13 The APU is concerned about the anonymity of pupils taking part in the survey and it is agreed that pupils' names should not appear on any of the materials used in their assessments or be known outside the school. The procedure which has been adopted ensures the anonymity of the pupils tested while allowing checks to be made on the data.

1.14 A two-stage system is used in which teachers are asked to enter on specially designed pupil data forms the date of birth and sex of each of the pupils selected for the sample. These forms, made up of sets of direct-copying paper, are so designed that one copy is wider than the others to allow the name of the pupil to be entered alongside the date of birth. This copy is retained by the school. On receipt of the other copies of the form containing only the date of birth and sex of each pupil the NFER allocates a pupil reference number to each entry and one copy now containing the reference number as well as date of birth and sex is returned to the school so that the number can be entered on the school's copy containing the names of the pupils. Each test and questionnaire booklet subsequently sent to a school has one of the reference numbers allocated to the selected pupils in that school printed in advance on the front page. Names are not required and the test data are linked only to a reference number. The only link between the pupil's name and reference number is held by the school. Thus the pupil's anonymity is not only preserved but also seen to be preserved.

1.15 It has also been agreed that schools and local education authorities will not be identified in any document or report produced by NFER for transmission to the DES, the Welsh Office, the DENI or for general publication.

Data collection

1.16 The NFER followed its normal procedure of asking local education authorities for permission to contact schools under their control.

1.17 This was given in all but six cases in which the authority felt there were particular factors which argued for exclusion of the schools. The schools were first contacted in July 1979, and were informed of the consultations which had already taken place with their LEAs and of the guaranteed anonymity of pupils, schools and LEAs. They were asked to agree to administer a test of about 50 minutes to some of the pupils in the age group.

1.18 Instructions for the testing were sent to schools about three weeks before the testing week and were followed by the tests themselves. Teachers were asked to make sure that each pupil completed the booklet allocated by a reference number to him or her. The way in which pupil reference numbers were allocated to the test booklets ensured that the 25 different written tests (see Chapter 3) were distributed at random throughout the sample of pupils. Testing was carried out in the week beginning 12 November 1979 and a further fortnight from the day of testing was allowed to test any pupil absent on that day.

1.19 Other information requested from the schools included the date of testing for each pupil or an indication of a pupil's absence or withdrawal, data concerning absenteeism and the numbers of pupils taking free school meals.

Appendix 2

Statistical significance

The meaning of statistical significance

1.1 The purpose of drawing a random sample is to allow statistical inferences to be made about the defined population from which it was taken. Different samples drawn from the same population are subject to variations in their characteristics, so that their mean scores differ both among themselves and from the mean of the population. The larger the sample, the more precise its mean will be as an estimate of the population mean.

1.2 If it is desired to compare the performance of pupils in different defined sub-populations (for example, pupils aged 15 years from Northern schools and pupils aged 15 years from Southern schools), then separate samples would be drawn from each sub-population. What is required is to decide whether any difference between the sample means reflects a real difference between the sub-population means, and the classical statistical significance test is designed to do this. The procedure is to calculate the probability that a difference in the sample means of the observed magnitude or higher would be found if the sub-populations in fact had the same means. If the probability of getting the obtained difference is low (e.g. 5 per cent or 1 in 20 chances) on the assumption that the sub-populations are the same, then the difference between the sample means is said to be statistically significant at that level of probability (i.e. at the 5 per cent level). Such a significance test may also be viewed as a device for providing evidence about the direction of the difference, so that a statistically 'significant' result is strong evidence that the difference between the sub-population means is in the same direction as that of the sample means. A 'non-significant' result simply fails to provide such evidence.

1.3 Thus, if a difference between two sample means is significant at the 5 per cent level this only means that, if there was no difference between the sub-populations from which the samples were drawn, such a difference could be expected to arise by chance between no more than 1 pair of samples out of 20 (i.e. 5 per cent). It follows that if 20 independent differences between sample means are tested at the 5 per cent level it is to be expected that one of them will be "significant" *even if there is no real difference* between the sub-populations sampled. This proviso should be particularly noted in the context of the data from the written tests and background variables where a very large number of significance tests have been carried out.

1.4 Statistical significance does not provide an indication of the educational significance of a difference between the defined populations. Thus, a statistically non-significant large difference between sample means may be more worthy of note for further investigation than a statistically significant small difference between sample means; the former needs to be supported statistically, but the latter might be of little interest educationally even if it was a real difference. Throughout this report therefore references are made to statistically significant results which must then be judged in relation to their possible educational significance and implications both of which are usually left to the reader.

The tests of significance used for this report

2.1 Throughout the analyses for this report statistical significance has been determined by computing the statistic $\bar{Z}$ described in Chapter 9 of *Fundamental statistics in psychology and education* by J P Guilford and B Fruchter, fifth edition, published in 1973 by McGraw-Hill. The standard error terms given by Guilford and Frutcher have however been modified to make allowance for the inflation (the "design effect") arising from the use of a stratified cluster sample rather than a simple random sample. The estimated design effect on the variance of the sub-category scores is 1.7 for the 1979 data and this has also been used as an estimate of design effect for the practical and attitude data. A detailed discussion of cluster sampling and design effect is to be found in *Survey sampling* by Leslie Kish, published in 1965 by Wiley.

Appendix 3

Practical testers

	School
Mrs A Behan	Castle Hill Girls' High School, Bolton.
Mrs H J Boyce	Crayford School, Crayford.
Mrs V Boyle	Dunmurry High School, Belfast.
E Davies	Altwood School, Maidenhead.
M Denning	Calder High School, Hebden Bridge.
F Foreman	Glan y Mor Comprehensive School, Llanelli.
R Gaunt	Berry Hill Secondary School, Coleford.
R W Horgan	Oldborough Manor School, Maidstone.
J G Howells	Codsall High School, Nr. Wolverhampton.
A G Kaye	Philippa Fawcett Mathematics Centre, London S.W.16.
F Kurley	Rowlinson Campus, Sheffield.
N Langdon	Smile Centre, London, W.10.
K Lorrison	Duchess's High School, Alnwick.
D McDermott	Carnhill High School, Londonderry.
R McDonald	Cantnil Comprehensive, Knowsley.
E Morgan	Edlington Comprehensive, Nr. Doncaster.
Mrs V Morgan	Falmer School, Falmer, Brighton.
R Nightingale	Ryehills School, Redcar.
H Pettman	Judgemeadow Community College, Evington, Leicester.
K Rastogi	Canon Palmer High School, Seven Kings, Ilford.
G Saltmarsh	Queen Elizabeth's School. Crediton.
P G Scott	Teachers' Centre, London E.17.
C Simpson	Richmond High School, Halesowen.
G Smart	Wolverhampton Teachers Centre.
T J Stannard	East Bergholt High School, Nr. Colchester.
B Thomas	Ysgol Aberconwy, Conwy.
B R Thomas	Montsaye School, Kettering.

Appendix 4

The attitude questionnaire

Notes on the statistical procedures

Development of the scales

[1] *Tests of Attainment in Mathematics in Schools,* Kyles, I and Sumner, R. Windsor: NFER. 1977.

1.1 The 34 statements to which pupils were asked to respond were selected on the basis of an earlier pilot study which had been carried out in the spring of 1979. Although some of the statements which formed the scales had been culled from published attitude scales, most were taken from the original TAMS study[1] during which pupils were asked to express their feelings toward mathematics by writing essays and completing unfinished sentences concerning those feelings. Consequently, the majority of the statements were spontaneously expressed opinions by pupils themselves and had been analysed previously for their relationship to one another. Sixty-four of these statements were administered to a sample of 269 pupils in 12 schools. The responses were then reanalysed, and the final selection and assignment of each statement to one of the scales were made on the basis of two criteria: a high correlation with other statements on the scale and a moderate level of discrimination among pupils.

[1] 'Coefficient Alpha and the internal structure of tests,' Cronbach, L. J. in *Psychometrika,* 1951, 16, 297 – 334.

1.2 The first criterion was concerned with the degree to which each statement correlated with others that appeared to refer to a similar aspect of attitude. In order to establish that all the items on the scale were tapping the same dimension of attitude, a factor analysis was made of the responses. Internal consistency of the individual scales was also examined by splitting each scale in every possible way and examining the correlation between one half and the other using the Cronbach Alpha coefficient[1]. These analyses were used as guides for choosing statements for the final reduced scales. Unless individual items were strongly related to others on the scale, they were dropped.

1.3 The second criterion was related to the distribution of responses. A disproportionate number of agreements or disagreements with any one statement would signal that the statement was not discriminating among pupils. Although such a response pattern may be interesting to report separately, such statements do not contribute to a scale which may be used to investigate the effect of attitudes on performance. In such a scale, it is the differences between pupils rather than their similarities that is of prime importance. For this reason, statements to which fewer than 15 per cent agreed or disagreed were dropped from the scale.

1.4 As a result of these analyses, 34 statements referring to the enjoyment, difficulty and utility of mathematics were chosen to appear in random order in one section of the questionnaire. In general, the statements reflected the name of the scale, i.e., most statements which were assumed to measure a predisposition to find mathematics difficult explicitly referred to some aspect of difficulty. This is not in strict accordance with questionnaire theory which counsels an equal proportion of positive and negative statements in order to avoid the possibility that the statements themselves may induce a tendency to respond in a particular fashion. This policy was not followed because the scales were not treated as entities but were intermeshed with one another and with non-scaled statements. It was assumed that such presentation would counteract any "response set" that might otherwise occur.

1.5 The 34 statements contained in the survey questionnaire had satisfied both criteria and were seen to measure three distinct aspects of attitude towards mathematics. However, this reduced set of items, when administered to the survey sample, yielded a different pattern of relationships from that achieved in the pilot study. A principal components analysis of the 34 responses indicated that difficulty, not enjoyment, was the principal factor, accounting for 28 per cent of the total variance. The next two factors, reflecting enjoyment and usefulness, accounted for another 11 per cent of the total variance. Furthermore, when a varimax factor rotation was performed, it was apparent that three statements correlated equally highly with both the utility and the difficulty factors, although semantically they appeared to reflect one or the other, while another statement correlated with both difficulty and enjoyment. Two other statements, expressing an attitude of boredom with mathematics, loaded on all three factors. Finally, two other statements did not load sufficiently highly on any one to be considered a valid measure of that factor.

1.6 As a result of these analyses, the scales were reconstituted. The four statements which correlated with all or none of the factors were dropped from the scales to be reported separately. Responses to another three were included on both the utility and the difficulty scales, while one statement was included on the difficulty and enjoyment scales.

Correlation of performance and attitude measures

2.1 Missing data is often a problem in the analysis of survey data. Respondents do not complete all the items or cannot furnish all the information required. Normally, such cases are eliminated from the computation of correlation coefficients. This results in a reduction in sample size, since only those cases with a complete set of values on the relevant variables are included. It may also lead to distortion of the final results if there is evidence of a consistent bias of response in those cases which are incomplete and, therefore, eliminated.

2.2 An alternative procedure exists in which missing values are replaced by arbitrary ones, often the mid-point value of the scale. This procedure has the advantage of including all the data in the analysis. Its disadvantage is that, by arbitrarily assigning a median score to a missing value, it reduces the variance of the scale and results in a regression to the mean.

2.3 After considering both procedures and examining the scripts themselves it was decided to assign mid-point scores to missing values on the scales. This decision was taken because of the number of pupils who stated that they were unfamiliar with one or more of the topics and, consequently, did not complete the judgement section for that topic.

2.4 The proportion of pupils who expressed unfamiliarity with a topic ranged from 32 per cent in response to an item on matrices, to 2 per cent in response to a computational item involving fractions. As a result, 45 per cent of the judgement scores (i.e., the sum of judgements of individual topics on each scale) were incomplete. If these scores were deleted from the analysis, it was probable that the final results would be distorted in favour of those pupils who were following a course including matrices or were more capable of generalising from specific examples.

2.5 A comparison of the results of both analyses showed little difference. The substitution of median values for missing ones did not alter mean scores to a significant degree. Although the correlation coefficients that resulted from the inclusion of all cases were slightly lower than those computed for complete cases only, the pattern of relationship remained substantially the same. It is concluded, therefore, that the results presented in tables 5.3–5.6 are valid despite the statistical manipulation of the scores.

2.6 On the other hand, because of the nature of the correction the size of the correlations are smaller than would normally occur. For comparison purposes, the correlation matrices that occurred when only the full sets of scores were considered are presented here.

Table A4.1   *Intercorrelation between the attitude measures and performance score among boys and girls.**

	General mathematics scales				Topic scales		
	Performance score	Enjoyment	Difficulty	Utility	Interest	Difficulty	Utility
Performance score	—	*16* 15	*−41* −45	*36* 28	*27* 10	*−69* −64	*42* 30
General enjoyment		—	*−58* −59	*56* 55	*54* 44	*−39* −38	*47* 48
General difficulty			—	*−72* −67	*−36* −27	*47* 51	*−40* −38
General utility				—	*45* 42	*−41* −36	*53* 52
Topic interest					—	*−38* −26	*64* 68
Topic difficulty						—	*−50* −45
Topic utility							—

Girls results in italic
Boys results in roman

*Because of the statistical method used (i.e., pairwise deletion of missing data), the correlations above are based on different numbers of cases, ranging from 229 to 408 in the case of girls, and from 240 to 458 in the case of boys.

Table A4.2 *Partial correlation coefficients between attitude measures with performance score controlled.*

	General mathematics scales			Topic scales		
	Enjoyment	Difficulty	Utility	Interest	Difficulty	Utility
General enjoyment	—	*−57* −59	*55* 53	*52* 43	*−39* −37	*45* 46
General difficulty		—	*−67* −63	*−29* −25	*29* 33	*−28* −29
General utility			—	*−39* −42	*−25* −25	*45* 47
Topic interest				—	*−28* −27	*60* 69
Topic difficulty					—	*−32* −35
Topic utility						—

Girls results in italic, n = 228
Boys results in roman, n = 238

Table A4.3 *Partial correlation coefficients between attitude measures and performance score (judgement of utility of topic item controlled)*

	General mathematics scales				Topic scales	
	Performance	Enjoyment	Difficulty	Utility	Interest	Difficulty
Performance score	—	*04* 00	*−29* −38	*18* 15	*00* 16	*−61* −60
Enjoyment scale		—	*−49* −50	*42* 40	*35* 17	*−21* −21
Difficulty scale			—	*−65* −60	*−15* −01	*34* 41
Utility scale				—	*17* 11	*−20* −17
Judgement interest					—	*−09* −07
Judgement difficulty						—

Girls results in italic, n = 228
Boys results in roman, n = 238

Appendix 5

5.1 Membership of the Monitoring Team

The members of the Mathematics Monitoring Team at the NFER responsible for carrying out the mathematics surveys are:

Mr D D Foxman (Leader)
Dr G J Ruddock (Deputy Leader)
Dr M E Badger
Mr R M Martini
Mr P Mitchell

5.2 APU Steering Group on Mathematics

Mr T A Burdett HMI (Chairman)	APU
Miss J L Atkin HMI	HM Inspectorate
Dr A W Bell	The Shell Centre for Mathematical Education, University of Nottingham
Miss M I Boland HMI	DENI
Mr D D Foxman	Leader, Mathematics Monitoring Team, NFER
Dr K Hart (from March 1981)	Centre for Science and Mathematics Education, Chelsea College, London.
Mrs J Holloway	Fairlight Middle School, Brighton
Mr I R Lloyd	HM Inspectorate (Wales)
Mr D J Maxwell	Education Adviser, North Tyneside
Mr G Saltmarsh (to March 1981)	Queen Elizabeth's School, Crediton
Mr P J Scott	Headmaster, City of Leeds School, Leeds
Dr A S Willmott (to March 1981)	NFER

5.3 Monitoring Services Unit (NFER)

Mrs B A Bloomfield (Head of Unit)
Mrs A Baker
Mrs M Hall
Miss E Evans (Secretary)

5.4 Monitoring Group (NFER)

Dr C Burstall (Chairman)
Mrs B A Bloomfield

Dr B H Choppin
Mr D D Foxman
Dr T P Gorman
Mr A N James
Mr B Sexton (Project Statistician)
Dr R Sumner
Dr A S Willmott

5.5 Members of the APU Consultative Committee

Professor J Dancy (Chairman)	School of Education, University of Exeter
Miss J E L Baird	Joint General Secretary, AMMA
Mr P Boulter	Director of Education, Cumbria (ACC)
Mr P J Casey	Deputy Director (Education and Training), (CBI)
Mr R G Cave	Senior Education Officer, Cambridgeshire
Mr H Dowson	Deputy Headmaster, Earl Marshal School, Sheffield (NUT)
Mr P J P Eley	National Confederation of Parent-Teacher Associations
Professor S J Eggleston	Department of Education, University of Keele
Mr A Evans (from April 1981)	Education Department, NUT
Mr D Fisher	County Education Officer, Hertfordshire (ACC)
Mr G S Foster	Headmaster, The Towers School, Ashford (NUT)
Mr G Hainsworth	Director of Education, Gateshead (AMA)
Mrs N Harrison	London Borough of Haringey (AMA)
Mr K S Hopkins	Deputy Director of Education, Mid-Glamorgan (WJEC)
Mrs J Hughes (to October 1980)	Director, Macmillan Publishers Ltd
Mr C Humphrey	Director of Education, Solihull (AMA)
Mr A Jarman (to April 1981)	Education Department, NUT
DR K Jones	Parent and Doctor, Sheffield
Mr T M Jones	Headmaster, Werneth Junior School, Oldham (NUT)
Mr J A Lawton	Chairman, Kent County Council (ACC)
Mr G M Lee	Doncaster Metropolitan Institute of Higher Education (NATFHE)
Mr S Maclure	Editor, Times Educational Supplement
Mrs R Mills (from January 1981)	Consultant Economist
Mr J G Owen (to January 1981)	Chief Education Officer, Devon
Mr M J Pipes (from December 1980)	Headmaster, City of Portsmouth School for Boys (NAHT)

Mr A M S Poole	Headmaster, Western School, Mitcham (NAS/UWT)
Dr W Roy	Headmaster, The Hewett School, Norwich (NUT)
Professor M D Shipman	Department of Education, University of Warwick
Miss A C Shrubsole	Principal, Homerton College
Mr F A Smithies	Assistant General Secretary (Education), (NAS/UWT)
Mr T P Snape	Headmaster, King Edward VI School, Totnes (SHA)
Miss R Stephen (to February 1981)	Association of Professional, Executive, Clerical and Computer Staff
Mr D M Wilkinson (to December 1980)	Headmaster, Wolgarston Comprehensive, Penkridge (NAHT)
Professor J Wrigley	School of Education, University of Reading
Mr A Yates	Director, National Foundation for Educational Research

Appendix 6

Note on the APU

The assessment of Performance Unit (APU) was set up in 1975 within the Department of Education and Science. It aims to provide information about national levels of performance in a number of curricular areas and across the full ability range.

The terms of reference of the APU are as follows:

> To promote the development of methods of assessing and monitoring the achievement of children at school, and to seek to identify the incidence of under-achievement.

Associated with these terms of reference are the following tasks:

- To identify and appraise existing instruments and methods of assessment which may be relevant for these purposes.

- To sponsor the creation of new instruments and techniques for assessment, having due regard to statistical and sampling methods.

- To promote the conduct of assessment in cooperation with local education authorities and teachers.

- To identify significant differences of achievement related to the circumstances in which children learn, including the incidence of under-achievement, and to make the findings available to those concerned with resource allocation within government departments, local education authorities and schools.

In developing its monitoring programme the APU has been concerned to reflect the breadth of the curriculum in schools and to display the full range of pupil performance. Many school subjects involve mathematical skills and concepts to some degree just as every part of the school curriculum depends upon and makes its own contribution to language development. In the same way scientific development is not solely the product of science teaching, nor does aesthetic awareness grow solely from formal instruction in art, music and drama.

The first APU surveys took place in 1978, in mathematics. English language monitoring began in 1979, and science monitoring in 1980. Monitoring of the first foreign language (French, German and Spanish) will begin in 1983. Although there is at present no commitment to monitor performance in any other areas, exploratory work is being undertaken to investigate the desirability and feasibility of assessing pupils' performance in the areas of aesthetic, physical and technological development. Some work has also taken place in the field of personal and social development, but it has been decided not to undertake national monitoring in this area.

The assessment procedures in mathematics are developed by the Mathematics Monitoring Team at the National Foundation for Educational Research. Their work is steered by a group consisting of teachers, advisers, teacher trainers, educational researchers and HMI, acting under the overall direction of the Heads of the Unit. The Secretary of State for Education and Science is advised about the work of the Unit as a whole by a Consultative Committee which is broadly representative of local authority and teacher associations, both sides of industry, parents, researchers and the education service generally. Advice about statistical matters and sampling strategy is provided by a Statistics Advisory Group.

The aim of the APU is to produce and make generally available national pictures of pupil performance. The Unit does not produce statements about the performance of individual children, schools or local education authorities. The results of the surveys are published regularly, in the form of reports, by Her Majesty's Stationery Office. This is the fifth report to be published, and is the second report on the mathematics performance of 15 year olds.

Leaflets about the work of the APU are available from the Department of Education and Science, Information Division, Room 2/11, Elizabeth House, York Road, London SE1 7PH.

Index

An asterisk against a paragraph reference indicates that a definition or explanation of the term can be found in that paragraph.

(Note: A denotes Appendix)

Printed in England for Her Majesty's Stationery Office
by Adams Bros. & Shardlow Ltd., Leicester
Dd 0698775 C 40 11/81